BOLLYWOOD OUTSIDER

A SUCCESS STORY

SUSHRUT ALMAST

BlueRose ONE.com
Stories Matter
NewDelhi • London

A Knowledge Millennium Positive Cinema Pvt Ltd Presentation
Publishers of Real Life Inspired, Success & Happiness products

BLUEROSE PUBLISHERS
India | U.K.

For permissions requests or inquiries regarding this publication, please contact:

BLUEROSE PUBLISHERS
www.BlueRoseONE.com
info@bluerosepublishers.com
+91 8882 898 898
+4407342408967

ISBN: 978-93-7018-945-4

Cover design: Yash Singhal
Typesetting: Namrata Saini

First Edition: January 2025

Message from Mr. Sandeep Marwah

I take this opportunity to congratulate Mr. Sushrut Almast for penning this wonderful book Bollywood Outsider-A Success Story which is an essential read for both aspiring filmmakers and seasoned professionals looking to refine their craft. This book is an expansive guide that covers the entire filmmaking process from pre-production to post-production. It serves as a one-stop resource for understanding the technical and creative aspects of making a film, presented in a way that is accessible and informative.

One of the book's greatest strengths lies in its comprehensive nature. It covers everything from camera techniques and lighting to sound design and editing, ensuring that readers gain a full understanding of the equipment and creative decisions involved in filmmaking.

Mr. Sushrut also emphasizes the importance of storytelling and structure, discussing how a filmmaker's choices in terms of framing, pacing, and tone directly influence the audience's experience. The book does not shy away from the complexities of filmmaking; it gives equal weight to the art and the science, making it an excellent manual for anyone who wants to understand how films are made on a deeper level.

In conclusion, this book is a treasure trove of knowledge for filmmakers who wish to understand the ins and outs of film production. I once again congratulate Mr. Sushrut and wish him all the best for the success of the book.

Sandeep Marwah
Chancellor AAFT University of Media and Arts

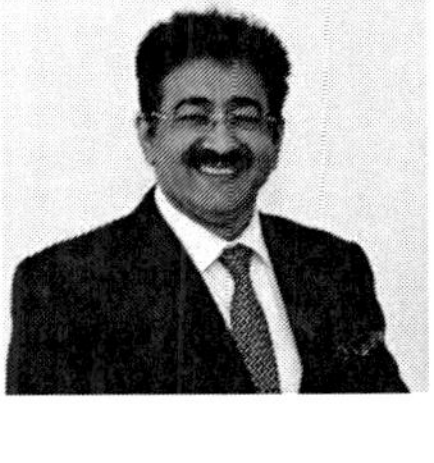

Message from Mr. Rakesh Bhatia

Good morning, everyone. I'm honored to be the guest of honor at the launch of Dr. Sushrut's book, 'Bollywood - outsider'

As I dig into the pages of this book, I was struck by Dr. Sushrut's unique perspective on the Indian film industry. The title, 'Bollywood Outsider' is thought-provoking, and the book lives up to its promise of offering a fresh, outside-in look at the world of Bollywood.

Dr. Sushrut's writing is engaging, informative, and insightful. The book is a must-read for anyone interested in understanding the complexities, challenges, and triumphs of the Bollywood ecosystem.

I'd like to congratulate Dr. Sushrut on this outstanding achievement. Your passion for storytelling, combined with your expertise and research, makes 'Bollywood Outsider' compelling read.

To the readers, I encourage you to explore this book, which offers a nuanced understanding of the Indian film industry. Dr. Sushrut's work will resonate with you, inspire you, and maybe even challenge your perceptions about Bollywood.

Once again, thank you for inviting me to be a part of this special morning. I wish Dr. Sushrut continued success, and I hope 'Bollywood Outsider' becomes a landmark book in its field. Cheers!

Rakesh Bhatia
Chairman
BGIL Films and Technologies Ltd

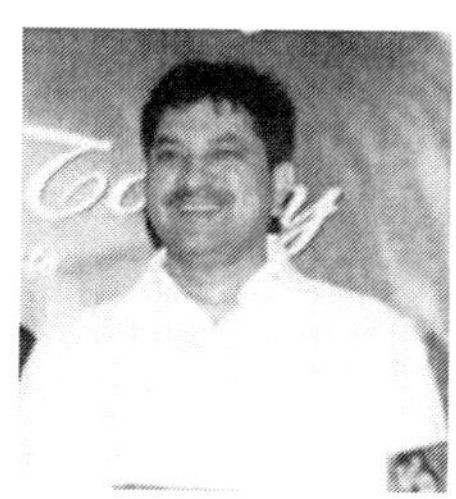

ABOUT THE AUTHOR

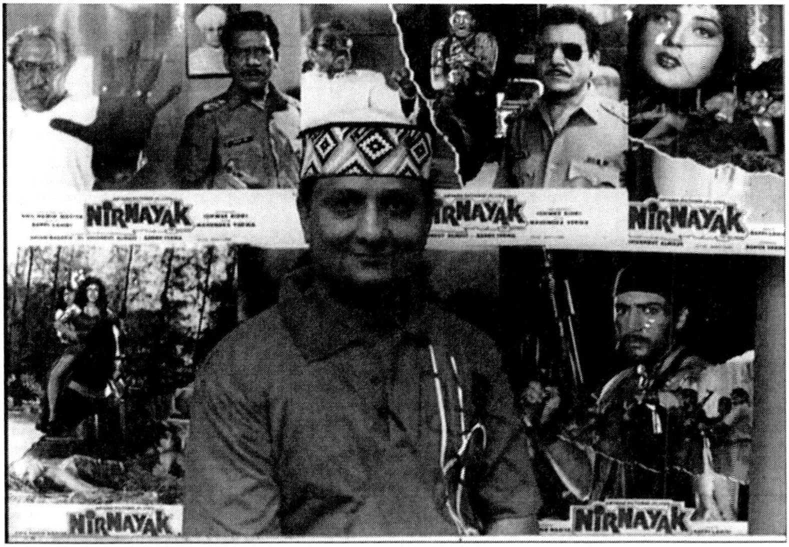

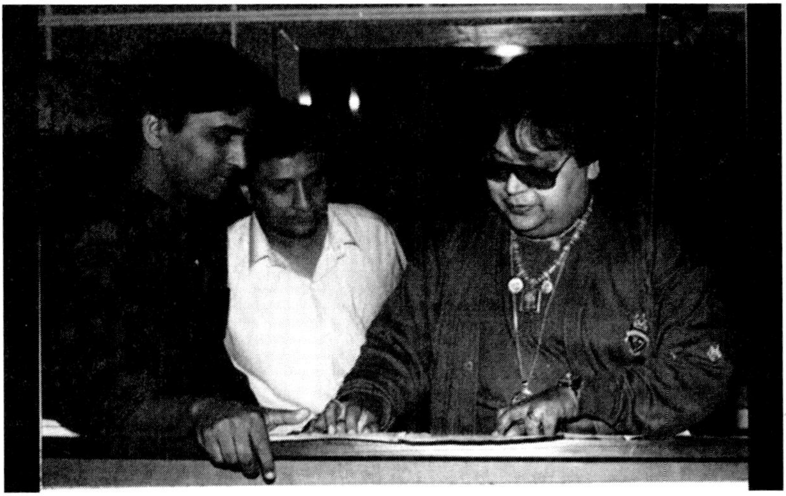

"I firmly believe that My India will lead our global family towards peace, prosperity and happiness."

-DR SUSHRUT ALMAST

ACADEMIC PURSUITS & ACHIEVEMENTS

Best All Rounder's Cup (Kanad House) - Birla Public School, Pilani, Rajasthan

MBBS, MD Radiodiagnosis MAMC, LHMC - Delhi University

Jyotish Alankar (Spl Int Medical Astrology)-Bhartiya Vidya Bhawan, Delhi

NCMF Certified (Dealer & Derivative Module)-National Stock Exchange of India

NIRNAYAK- The Decider (!997-98)-Bollywood Film Producer (Member IMPPA)

Chairman & Managing Director-Knowledge Millennium Positive Cinema P LTD

Founder & Chairman (Not for Profit)-Sukhi Sansar–Holistically Healthy India

Co-Founder & Chairman (Not for Profit)-KRRISSH–Reinventing Vedic Wisdom

Co-Founder Trustee & Gen Admin-Physicians Forum of India – (Not For Profit)-Empowering Doctors For A Healthy India

Ganesha-Excellence in Leadership-Author (Best Seller)

PROFILE

A dynamic & multifaceted individual with diversified professional knowledge ranging from the field of **medical sciences**, **media arts, finance** and a compelling drive to comprehend the complexities of **vedic** sciences and holistic life management solutions.

His venture into a wide & unrelated range of activities forced him to find a reason of his such diversified ventures. After much probing it was Vedic Astrology which solved his queries of his life activities. As Vedic Astrology is based on the theory of Karma and rebirth he developed deep interest in the mysteries of life and started studying the various aspects of the vedic sciences. His studies and research made him realize that the study of the self - who am I ? and my relationship to my surroundings , the science of selfology was the most important to lead a happy and successful life.

His literary work is focussed on inspirational, success and happiness themes based on real life events.

contact email of author:
sushrut.knowledgemillennium@gmail.com

Subscribe @youtube
@nirnayakmovie7461
@bollywoodmusicmainaurmasti8106
@kishoremainaurmasti1554
@krrissh587
@sukhisansar853
@physiciansforumofindia7578 (only for medical professionals)

ACKNOWLEDGEMENTS

No task is ever accomplished, goals achieved without the guidance, support, blessings of well wishers.

The success of both; the film **Nirnayak – The Decider** and the book Bollywood Outsider – A Success Story is a result of these well wishers and their contributions need to be mentioned, appreciated and thanked.

I thank film Co producer **Shyam Bagaria**, film director **Anil Wasia** my school friends who despite all frictions made **Nirnayak – The Decider** happen.

Thanks to **Ashok Verma** who joined us as co producer and reposed faith in us at the time of severe financial constraints.

Thanks to **Adarsh Gupta**, Director Liberty Shoes for giving the film infilm advertisement to promote their brand Force 10. Thanks to **Rajiv Gupta** for introducing me to Adarsh Gupta.

Thanks to **Subhash Ghai** promoter Mukta Arts for not forcing us to release Amrish Puri on shooting dates blocked with us.

Thanks to **Jawahar Lal Bafna** and **Sudhakar Bokade** for giving us essential tips on film production.

Thanks to **Dinesh Gandhi** for guiding us in film distribution.

Thanks to **IMPPA** – Indian Motion Pictures Producers Association for helping us in drafting contracts and agreements with cast, crew and film distributors and helping us resolve disputes amicably with various stake holders and their associations.

Thanks **to Kamal Sadanah, Indrani Banerjee, Om Puri, Ishwar Bidri** and other cast and crew members for withdrawing the Lab letters and forgoing their dues in the interest of film release.

Thanks to **Amrish Puri** for not demanding a increase in renumeration when he was commanding a 20X market price on what we had signed him for. In fact the major factor in worldwide release of the film and its success was the huge popularity which Amrish Puri and Om Puri enjoyed among the masses and their clash scenes and dialogues.

Thanks to **Bappi Lahiri** who never let us feel that we are first timers and Bollywood Outsiders and inspired us at every step.

Thanks to **Udit Narayan** for his support "Sir, lets record the song, don't worry about my renumeration. He was pleased to get a post dated cheque when we were short of money.

Thanks to Film Trade Magazines, **Film Information, Cinema Cinema**, in particular **Taran Adarsh** of **Trade Guide** for guiding us to take best advantage of industry magazines publicity and promoting our advertisements on post dated cheques.

Thanks to the **entire cast and crew** of Nirnayak – The Decider who stood with us during the ups and downs we faced during the making of the film.

Thanks to **Sunil Manchanda** of **Nu Count Chit Fund** to award me the first chit whenever I needed money.

Thanks to **Dinesh Bhaisahab** and **Rajiv Khandelwal** from my almamater Birla Public School, Pilani, Rajasthan to help us financially in emergency.

Thanks to **Shri B K Sood** Principal Birla Public School Pilani for appreciating our efforts in school assembly and encouraging us by distributing the audio cassette of Nirnayak among school students.

Thanks to my parents **Dr Sansar Chand Almast** and **Dr Sushila Almast** for breaking their FDs to support my project and for all adventures and experiments I undertook in my life.

How many women would part with their jewellery to support a film project by her husband. **Most importantly thanks to my wife Annu** for lending me her jewellery which I pledged with Federal Bank to avail funds.

All mighty God who gave me this ability of multitasking in unchartered territories, enjoying the thrills and challenges of medical radio-diagnosis, cinema, share markets, practical Vedanta including medical astrology and converting non profitable assets into money churners.

DEDICATED TO

My parents Surgeon–Dr Sansar Chand Almast & Gynaecologist–Dr Sushila Almast for their unflinching faith and support all along my foray into the unchartered territories of medical radio-diagnosis, finance, cinema, practical Vedanta including medical astrology.

Regret not being able to spend quality time with my family parents Dr Sansar Chand Almast, Dr Sushila Almast, spouse Annu, children Aastha, Aatraye & Charak between 1993 & 1997.

EDITOR'S NOTE

As the editor of this book, I must commend the author on crafting an engaging and thought-provoking manuscript. The writing style is captivating, with vivid storytelling and a clear passion for the subject. The elements of hard work and dedication remain persistent in the book, making it highly motivational and inspiring for the readers.

I look forward to seeing its positive impact on readers.

PREFACE

I love content creation because I feel that the experiences I have gained from this world make me feel complete and contented within myself. I feel indebted to the world for this. I want to return my experiences in an assimilated form back to the world for it to benefit from them.

The need for writing this book arose with the desire to share the challenges, adventures, obstacles faced by the first-time commercial cinema producers with no God Father in Bollywood and also serve as a guide to the means to overcome these obstacles and achieve ultimate success in the world of cinema for profits.

There was also a demand for a guide for those who want to enter commercial cinema space for the first time by some members of the Producers Group on LinkedIn which I was a member. However, I am no more on LinkedIn.

The need for writing this book arose with a desire to make cinema lovers aware of these behind the scene challenges, adventures and obstacles.

Any industry does change with the passage of Time and upgrading of technology but the fundamental principles always remain the same. Book provides insight of Commercial Cinema – Cinema for Profit.

Cinema lovers to experience risks and challenges in Commercial Cinema.

How risks can be minimised and profits increased.

Past Present and Future of Hindi Cinema.

Nepotism and Vanshvad in Bollywood, causes and solutions. Outsiders can pierce the wall of Insiders.

Bollywood to overtake Hollywood in terms of content and revenue. How?

Gain experience with a small budget regional cinema commercial film.

How to face challenges & achieve success in a world dominated by insiders, nepotism, Vanshvad.

How nepotism, Vanshvad, in particular Khan Kapoor nepotism, has not only destroyed all india talent but also produced mediocre content and anti-Hindu, anti-Indian culture narratives. Variable vs fixed factors in Commercial cinema.

Three ways Bollywood would get rid of Insider, Nepotism Vanshvad from Top10 Bollywood Actors.

Bollywood Directors, Producers, Writers, will stop slavery of Khans Kapoors and give good content films to Outsiders.
Pan Indian South Hindi Film Stars storm into Bollywood Top 10 Heroes.

Young India Boycott Insider, Nepotism films and watch Outsiders All IndiaTalent.

A Talented Chaiwala, Bus Conductor, Farmer as Hero No1 of Bollywood.

We have achieved this in Politics, Cricket, South-Indian Cinema Rajnikanth Yash.

Having been a successful multitasker throughout my life with forays into medical profession, astrological consultancy, share broking and trading, a brief stint at building construction, converting NPAs, non-performing assets into profitable products, film production and now film script writing and authoring books, I can easily say that the most difficult profession is commercial film production, cinema for profit.

Commercial cinema is all about making money, cinema for profit and a budget filmmaker has to tread his path very, very carefully.

The film finances, revenues, source of income, expenditure need to be finalized even before the first word of the script is written.

And finally, I would definitely like to read The Wonder, the success story of Kantara, a film made with a budget of 10 to 12 crores and grossing more than 400 crores at the box office.

CONTENTS

CHAPTER 1

The Proposal

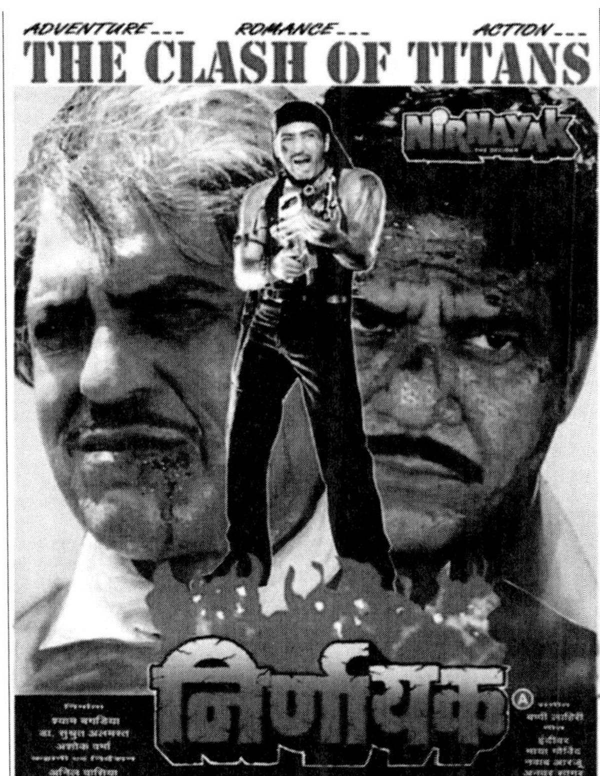

ARYAMA PICTURES (P) LTD PRESENTS

NIRNAYAK

Starring : · *Kamal Sadanah* · *Indrani Banerjee* · *Trishna* · *Rakesh bedi* *Maya Alagh* · *Jaya Mathur* · *Aprajita* · *Deepak Shirke* · *Shiva* · *Mahender Verma* · *Rubina* · *Dev Malhotra* · *Brij Gopal* · *Om Puri and Amrish Puri* ; **Introducing :** ***Neeraj Sharma & Baby Aastha***

Produced by	**Story & Directed by**	**Music**
Shyam Bagaria *Dr. Sushrut Almast* *Ashok Verma*	*Anil Wasia*	*Bappi Lahiri*

Lyrics
Indeevar, Maya Govind, Anwar Sagar, Nawab Arzoo

Cinematography	**Dialogues**	**Screen Play**
Ishwar Bidri	*Anil-Anando*	*Anando Roi*

Choreography
· *Rekha Chinni Prakash* · *Nimesh Bhatt* · *Habiba*
Action : *Mahender Verma* **Editing :** *Naresh* · *S. Ambasta*
Audiography : *Ashfaq* **Costumes :** *Neeta Malhotra*
Stills : *Anand Verma* ***P.R.O.*** : *Raju Karia* **Art :** *Madhu Kamle*

Assistants
Direction : Raju Rathi, Shalina, Ravinder
Sound : Arif; **Action** : Balu, Prem
Make-up : Krishna ; **Art** : Somnath
Editing : Govind Dubey

Publicity Printers & Designers : *Bhumica Printing Services*
Processed at : *ADLABs* ***Special Effects :*** *Cine Magic*
Songs Recorded at : *Filmistan, Sunny Super sound, Sahara*
Playback singers : *Kumar Sanu, Udit narayan, Babul Supriyo, Alka Yagnik, Rema Lahiri, Sharon Brabhakar & Bappi Lahiri*
Records on : *Ultra Series* ***Dressman :*** *Javed*
Production Controller : *Ravi Tripathi* ***Production manager :*** *B.G. Tripathi*
Make-up : *Vijay* **Re Recording :** *H. Ghosh (Raj Kamal)*

SYNOPSIS

Neelam, the beauty queen of the law college is a mischievious girl by nature. She likes to take up challenges. She decides to titilate the college students during her performance on the annual day function. Though she succees with flying colors but unfortunately her pranks take a different dimension. A group of daredevil students loose their sense and foreget the college decoram to the extent that they kidnap Neelam in a collective manner.

The news of kidnapping catches like a wild fire not only to that city but throughout the state cos **Neelam** happens to be the daughter of the Minister of the state - **Mr. Pradhan Des Pandey**. The state police department and the press are put on alert.

But **Neelam** is alive, though far away from the city - in a jungle. Her savior Suraj is a self - employed law graduate who prefers the job of horse training over law practice.

Despite all much needed hospitality which Suraj has accorted to **Neelam, Neelam** still refuses to accept him as her savior and doubts him to be the real kidnapper. This misgiving was enough for Neelam to sneak out of **Suraj's** farm cottage. But Suraj comes her rescue again in time; and becomes her savior for the second time as she was confronted by the kidnappers again. Now **Neelam** has to believe **Suraj,** so does she. And so does she loose her heart out to **Suraj**.

Their love not only becomes the talk of the town but it spreads throughout the state just like the news of her kidnapping. **Mr. Pradhan Desh Pandey** and his son **Vikram** cannot accept the fact that his daughter Neelam is getting along with a commoner. Vikram, Neelam's brother decides to hit back but all his plans and arguements with **Neelam** boomerang on Vikram when **Neelam** proclaims **Suraj** to be the love of life publically.

Vikram cannot take this open huminiation and decides to take the revenge. Infatuated by **Suraj** - sister and having that attitude of – taking away **Suraj** sister as he thinks **Suraj** has wrested his sister, **Vikram** decides to kidnap **Manisha, Suraj** sister but her kidnapping turns into a disaster. Due to unforseen circumstances **Vikram** finds himself compelled enough to kill all other family members except **Suraj** who happens to be absent at the time of abduction.

Suraj comes back home. He is confronted by the dead bodies lying all around. There is no eivdence except the car number of the abductor.

The number of the car leads **Suraj** to Mumbai. By making sundry official enquiries **Suraj**'s suspicion about **Vikram** gets confirmed. **Suraj** goes to **Vikram**'s house to have a man-to-man dialogue with him but to his surprise, **Vikram** even refuses to recognise him and **Suraj** is thrown out of **Vikram**'s house.

While in America, **Neelam** comes to know about her father's ploy to get her married and thus she immediately flies back to India. Back to her college, she comes to know about the massacre having taken place at **Suraj**'s house, she desperately tries to look for **Suraj** but **Suraj** has left no traces behind.

Here, in Mumbai, Suraj confronts **Pradhan Desh Pandey** in public. To avoid the embaracing situation, **Pradhan Desh Pandey** the politician, plays it diplomatic and invites **Suraj** to his residence. **Suraj** accepts the invitation - though oblivous of the trap that he is walking in.

The next morning, the Mumbaiates wake up to an electrifying news that a terrorist (**Suraj**) has been captutred from the Minister's residence.

The case being a sensitive one, is handed over to the most dynamic efficient and honest police inspector - Inspector **Nanak**. Inspector **Nanak** incidently happens to be the same inspector who was given **the** charge of rescuing **Neelam** from the kinappers and is therefore well aware of the love between **Surraj** and **Neelam** and realises that **Suraj** been falsely implicated as a terrorist by **Pradhan Desh Pandey** to get rid of him. He helps the innocent **Suraj** in getting freed from the jail.

With the help of **Suman** (**Nanak**'s Sister), **Suraj** succeeds in picking up one of **Vikram**'s crony who after having been hammered properly admits that **Manisha** was unable to endure the rape attempt of **Vikram** and committed sucide.

"AN EYE FOR AN EYE" and 'ATOOTH FOR A TOOTH **Suraj** decides instinctively.

With his family distroyed and his dreams shattered **Suraj** sees REVENGE as his sole purpose of his life. He kills the culprits and finds his love Neelam in his arms.

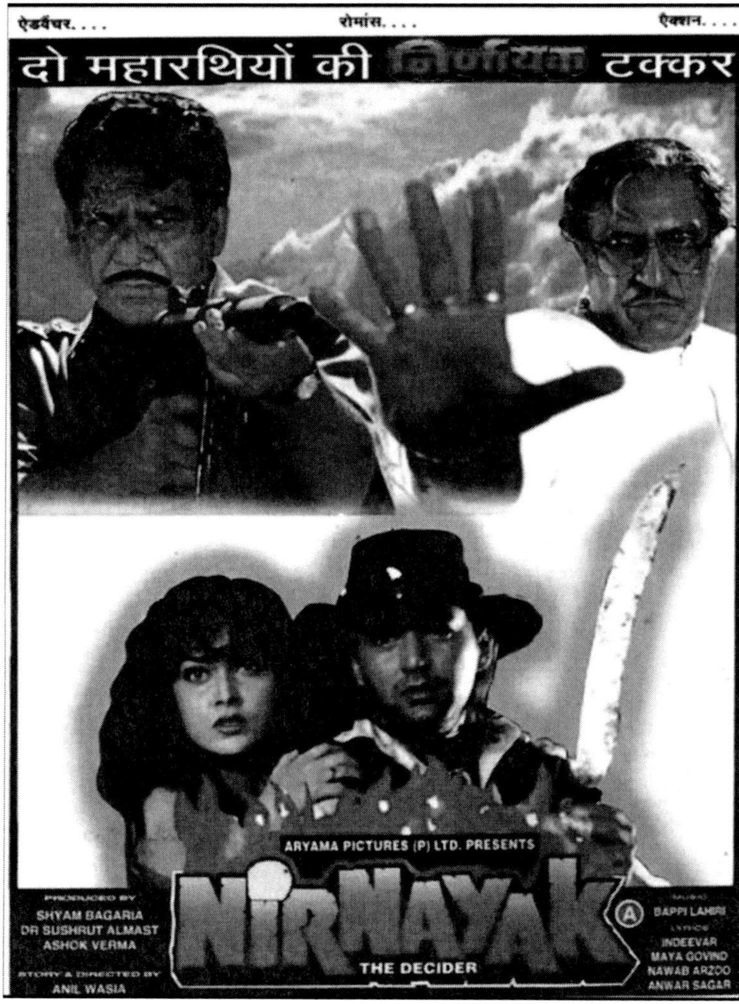

So, it all started on a Fine Sunday in January 1989, when a dear school friend Anil Wasia came to meet me and asked me if I would like my daughter Aastha to act in a Bollywood film.

Anil was pursuing a law degree at the Delhi Law College and simultaneously doing a course in acting from the National School of Drama.

I had just finished my MBBS and MD in Radio-diagnosis from the Delhi University and had set up a diagnostic centre at Kamla Nagar, Delhi.

Anil said that he was in the midst of writing a Bollywood film script in which there was a role of a small girl and Aastha would fit into the role.

I was fascinated by Bollywood films since childhood. Being an overactive child, my parents, who had a good surgical and gynaecological practice Delhi Clinic Nursing Home, used to send me to the Amba Cinema in North Delhi, Sabji Mandi nearby on Sundays to keep me busy in watching films at the theatre.

My father's surgical assistant Mr. Nigam had a brother who was a ticket checker at the Amba Cinema and would give me a seat at the box to watch the film.

As I grew up, I was sent to the Birla Public School, Pilani, a boarding school in class 7th. During the holidays, when I used to come home – on the first day itself, it was a regular practice for me to go to Connaught Place and watch all four shows at the Connaught Place Cinemas of Regal, Rivoli, Golcha and Plaza and watch all four films in a single day.

Even during the school tours waiting at the railway stations, If the train was even one hour late, me and my friends would enter a nearby cinema and watch the movie even for half an hour.

Also, cinema attracted me as there you are creating something which would remain in the world long after you are no more and therefore, I promised Anil that my daughter Aastha would play the role of the girl child in the movie he was about to make.

CHAPTER 2

Vyakul to Nirnayak

Exactly one year later in January 1990, Anil was back with a bound film script titled **Vyakul.**

During this one year, he had worked as an assistant director to **Vinod Pandey** in **Sach** and to **Shashilal Nair** in **Angaar**.

Anil, along with Anando Roi had written the film script of Vyakul
Anando Roi was an alumnus of the Film Institute Pune.

But this time Anil came with a different proposal.

Yes, as promised he had a role of the girl child for Aastha.

But along with that he asked me to help him with an initial sum of rupees 5 Lakhs to launch the film. The budget of the film as projected by Anil was 60 Lakhs and the lead stars included **Sunny Deol** and **Pooja Bhatt.**

FILM INFORMATION

BOMBAY SATURDAY 23rd May, 1992 PRICE Rs. 15/- VOL. XIX NO.

LAUNCHED ON 21ST MAY - MARATHON SHOOTING SCHEDULE FROM 10TH JUNE

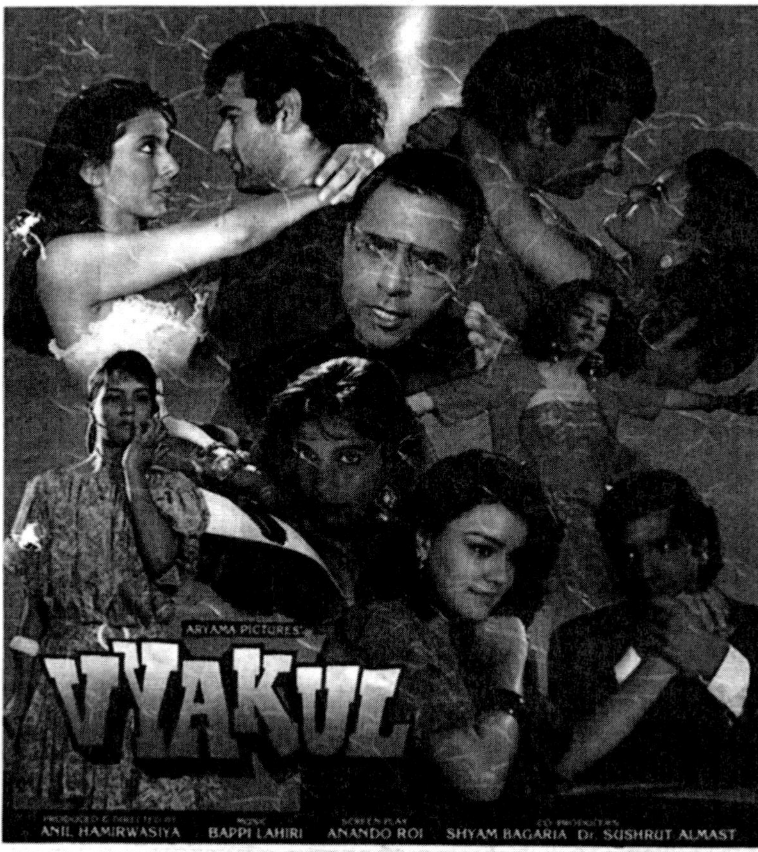

Issued by : **ARYAMA PICTURES PVT. LTD.,** 9, Shanti Bhuvan, 1st Floor, Chapel Lane, Santacruz (W), Bombay-400 054. Phone: **649- 1802**

Publicity: **PUNEET KHARE**

Trade Guide

40T

Glorious

GRAND DIWALI ATTRACTION

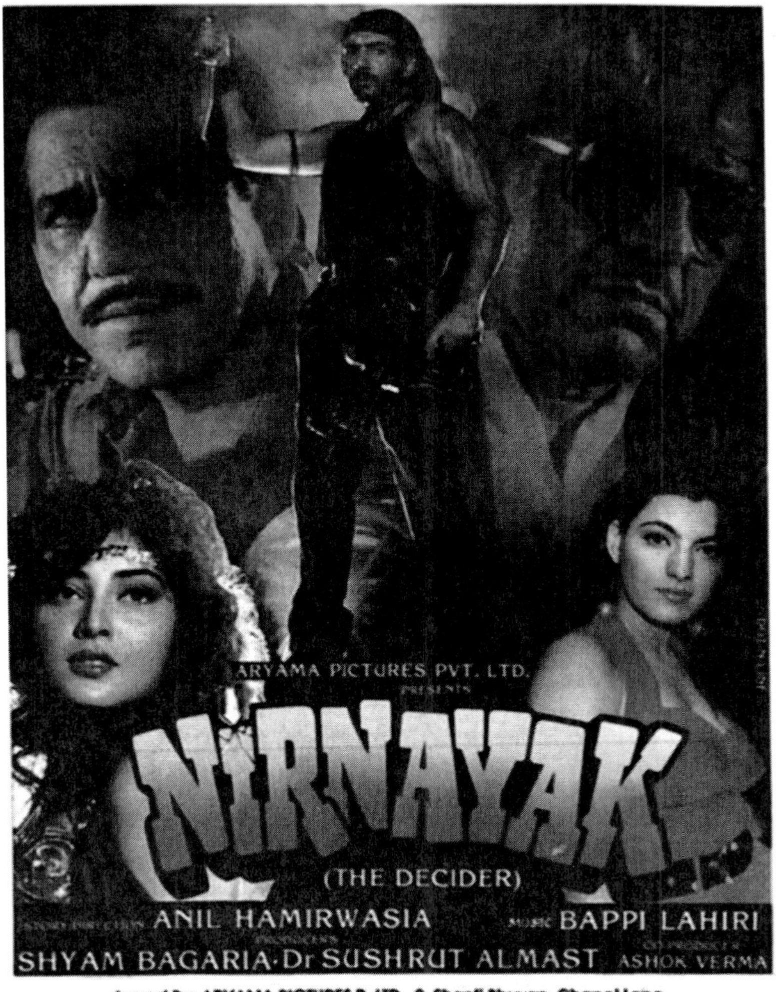

Issued By: ARYAMA PICTURES P. LTD., 9, Shanti Bhuvan, Chapel Lane, Santacruz (W.), Bombay-400 054. © 6491802.

P.R.O.: RAJOO KARIYA 62

He also promised to give me the title of Co-producer to me and he informed me that once the film went on floor with some initial scenes shot after the announcement, the distributor would join in to fund the project.

I thought over it and decided to include another friend, our school friend **Shyam Bagaria** who lived in Calcutta to join in as a Co producer.

Coincidentally, all three of us, Anil, Shyam and myself were from the same school, Birla Public School, Pilani.

All three of us had professional degrees. While, Anil was a lawyer by profession, Shyam was an engineer from BITS Pilani and myself a doctor radiologist from Delhi University. None of us had any contacts in Bollywood and zero experience of film production.

Shyam agreed to join me as Co producer but it was made explicitly clear to Anil that we were just helping him as friends and that we had no intention to turn Producers.

A Production Company by the name of **Aryama Pictures Private Limited** was registered in Delhi with the three of us as promoter directors.

Funds were provided to Anil to go ahead with the film project Vyakul.

Anil went to Bombay and set up the film project.

But the main leads were now **Ravi Behl** and **Sucheta**, a newcomer. The lead villain was **Ajit-The Lion.**

The other cast included **Tinu Anand** and **Johnny Lever.**

The launch was announced with an advertisement in the film trade magazines and press releases.

The Mahurat shot was scheduled at the Filmistan Studios and the event was attended by music director Bappi , producer Jawaharlal Bafna, Punit Esshar among others. Myself and Shyam Bagaria attended the Mahurat function along with Aastha and then we went back to our respective cities of Calcutta and Delhi.

Anil informed us that he had started shooting scenes for the film and that shortly they would be signing contracts with the distributors.

Around June 1991, I received a letter from Anil that he was very depressed and that no distributor had come forward to buy the film and that I should do something about it.

On his repeated request, I decided to visit Bombay in June 1992 and see for myself what all he had done till now.

I saw the five scenes he had shot and was impressed by his directorial capabilities.

I called Shyam and explained him the situation.

Shyam and me were also passing through an embarrassing situation.

Our family and friend were constantly inquiring about when the film would be released.

We had been trained at our school to fight all odds, take the bullet in the chest and not run away from any situation.

It had become a matter of self-respect and prestige for both of us.

We decided to invest and take over the project and manage the project as fulltime producers of the film.

Vyakul would be shelved.

Anil would no longer remain a producer and would just be a director of the film.

The name of the film was changed to NIRNAYAK - The Decider. The new star cast included Kamal Sadanah as the hero and Indrani Banerjee as the lead heroine. Indrani Banerjee was a winner of the Filmfare actress competition along with Sonali Bindre and Divya Dutta.

Star cast also included Rakesh Bedi, Om Puri and Amrish Puri and introducing Neeraj Sharma and Baby Aastha. Nirnayak – The Decider went on floors in March 1993.

CHAPTER 3

Consulting Senior Film Producers

At this stage, I suggested Anil and Shyam that we meet some senior producers and seek their guidance.

We first met **Jawaharlal Bafna** of the film **Ghar Ghar Ki Kahani** fame to seek his guidance.

Jawaharlal Bafna had two points of advice.

Firstly, the money you want to invest in a film, are you willing to put kerosene oil and burn the money?

If yes, go ahead.

Filmmaking is a very risky business, with films getting shelved at various stages of production. **An incomplete or unreleased film in theatres is a 100% loss.**

For various reasons, even censored films sometimes do not see the light of the day.

Films released in theatres rarely recover, the money invested, most being either flop or below average.

His other advice was never to dishonour a cheque issued to an actor or a technician. Artists are very emotional people. You tell them frankly that you are not in a position to pay and request to take payment later or against lab letter and they will happily agree, but never allow a cheque issued to be dishonoured.

Otherwise, they get upset and may not even cooperate and perform to their best or give you dates.

We also met Sudhakar Bokade of the film Sajan fame who liked the film script and suggested to have Shahrukh Khan and Kajol in the main lead.

Shahrukh Khan would come for about 20 lakhs while Kajol would charge about 10 lakhs.

Sudhakar Bokade was willing to finance the entire film in case Shahrukh Khan and Kajol were the main leads.

We discussed Sudhakar Bokade's proposal.

I was against such a move for various reasons.

For one, as per industry feedback, the source of fund was suspicious.

Secondly, taking Shahrukh Khan and Kajol entailed the risk of the project going out of our hands.

With the big banners Shahrukh Khan and Kajol were working, there was every likelihood that we would have problem handling them and completing our film and they could deny us dates in favour of established producers.
Anil and Shyam agreed to my logic and reasoning and therefore, we decided to continue with Kamal Sadanah and Indrani Banerjee as the main leads.

Some producers also advised us to first make a small budget regional film, a Bhojpuri or Punjabi film, gain experience before venturing into the world of Bollywood.

CHAPTER 4

Mahurat Shot

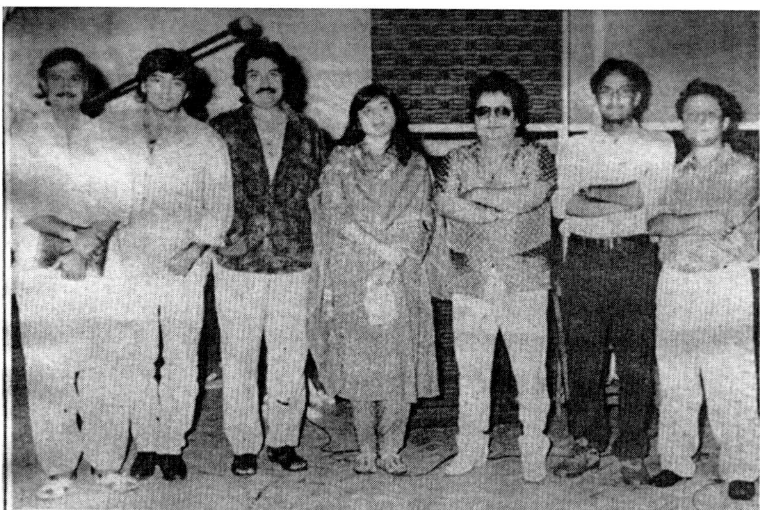

At the third song recording of Aryama Pictures' 'Nirnayak' at Sunny Super Sound are seen, from left, lyricist Nawab Arzoo, Kamal Sadanah, Kumar Sanu, Alka Yagnik, Bappi Lahiri, director Anil Wasia and producer Dr. Sushrut Almast.

Mahurat is considered to carry a special significance in Bollywood where almost every factor is a variable factor carrying very high risk.

Mahurat - auspicious time, Numerology, astrology – have a great say.

Usually, the Mahurat shot takes place at the shoot location at an auspicious time, with Ganesh Vandana, Pooja and the breaking of the coconut.

But during Nirnayak – The Decider, the Mahurat was with the recording of the song titled Tod do Diwar penned by Indivar with music and voice rendered by Bappi Lahiri.

Bollywood Film making being a high-risk business for all stakeholders, numerology and astrology plays a crucial role.

Actors change their name, add alphabets, wear precious stones like Neelam, blue, sapphire, panna, green, Emerald and diamond in particular, which represent the main planets governing the success of film industry.

Saturn is for popularity among masses, Mercury for communication and Venus for entertainment.

Every event is noted as auspicious or inauspicious.

In case of Nirnayak -The Decider, a few other things happened while erecting a cottage set in the film city.

The first day was marked with the roar of a tiger and passing of a snake on the sets.

Both these events are considered to be auspicious for the starting of any film and success of the film.

In an industry where less than 10% of movies which go to floor are lucky to be released in theatres, while the rest 90% are shelved at different stages of shooting after going on floor and some remain in the box even after obtaining a censor certificate, it is no wonder that mahurat, astrology, numerology, and palmistry play a big role.

These events bore a great significance for the making and box office success of NIRNAYAK – The Decider, giving us a lot of confidence.

CHAPTER 5

Lyrics and Songs

Songs are an essential part of any Bollywood film and a great contributor to its success.

Since I have already mentioned regarding the recording of the song Tod do Deewar as the mahurat shot, let me further share the details of the songs of Nirnayak.

6 songs in total were recorded out of which five songs were picturized.

The details of the songs are as follows.

Music director Bappi Lahiri.

Song 1 **Tod Do Dewar** Lyrics Indivar Singer Bappi Lahiri

Song 2 **Teri Hansi Ne** Lyrics Anwar Sagar Singers Kumar Sanu and Alka Yagnik.

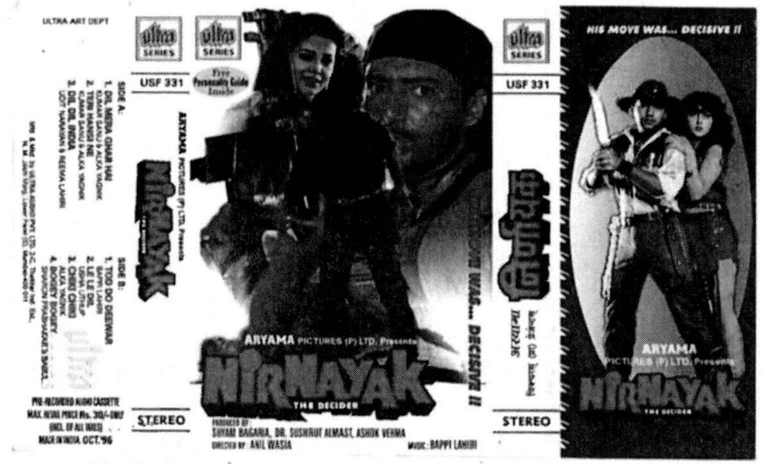

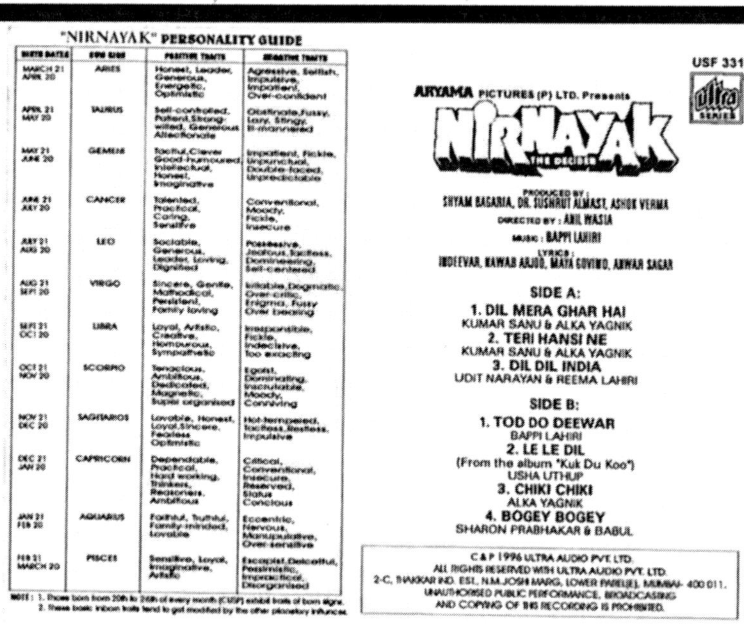

Song 3 **Dil Mera Ghar** Lyrics Nawab Arzoo Singer Kumar Sanu and Alka Yagnik.

(17)

GOVERNMENT OF INDIA

ALL INDIA RADIO, BOMBAY

AN AGREEMENT made the.....14th.....................day of...May 94......(one thousand nine hundred and eighty..Ninety four...............**BETWEEN** the President of India (hereinafter referred to as "The Government" which expression shall, where the context so admits, include his successors and assigns) on the one part and M/s. ARADHANA PICTURES PVT. LTD. .... having his/their office at ..9. SHANTI BHUVAN, CHAPEL LANE, SANTACRUZ(W), BOMBAY-400 054 (hereinafter referred to as "The Producer" which expression shall where the context so admits, include his legal representatives and assigns) on the other part.

WHEREAS the Government has under its control a number of Broadcasting Stations in India (hereinafter referred to as The "Station" which expression shall include Broadcasting Stations in India) which may thereafter come under the control of Director General, All India Radio, hereinafter called as "The Director General."

AND WHEREAS the ownership and/or control of the authors', composers' and performers' rights in the songs occuring in and forming part of the films hitherto produced and those to be produced by the said producer is vested in the producer.

AND WHEREAS the Government acting in the premises through the said Director General desires to acquire for the purpose of broadcasting by vocal performances and by the playing of gramophone records the authors,' composers' and performers' rights in the songs occuring in and forming part of the film hitherto produced and those to be produced by the said producer.

AND WHEREAS, in the consideration of the payments hereby agreed to be made by the Government, the producer has agreed to assign the aforesaid rights to the Government.

NOW IT IS HEREBY AGREED AS FOLLOWS:—

(1) In this agreement the word "song" means the arrangement of words sung with or without musical accompaniment as per copy supplied by the producer.

(2) In the agreement, the word "India" shall have the same meaning as contained in sub-clause (*c*) of Clause (28) of section 3 of the General Clauses Act 1897 as adapted by the Adaptation of Laws Order 1950.

(3) That all the songs which have been used or may in future be used by the producer in films produced by him from time to time may be broadcast by the Director General from All or any of the Stations.

(4) In cases where the songs have been, or may be recorded and the manufactures rights are, or may be vested in the producer the broadcast of such records under this agreement will not give rise to any claim by the producer.

(5) The Producer warrants that he holds the authors', composers' and performers' rights in the songs used in the film produced by him that no other person, firm or company has any interest in the right hereby assigned to the Government and that none of the said songs (nor any part of any of them) is in any way a violation or infringement of any subsisting copy-right of the world.

(6) The Producer undertakes to keep the Government at all times fully indemnified in respect of the consequences following upon any or all actions, proceedings, claims, demands and expenses whatever which may be brought against or suffered or incurred by the Government in consequences of any breach of any such work as aforesaid is an infringement of any rights of any other person or is libellous or slanderous or controversial or otherwise in any way arising out of the exercise of the right hereby granted.

(7) In consideration of the rights granted by the said producer, the Government agrees to pay a sum of Rupee Two per song per broadcast, the amount being paid in *annual* instalments to the producer and the receipt under the signature or seal of the said Producer shall operate as good and sufficient discharge in respect of all moneys payable hereunder. The radiation of any one item once from one transmitter or once simultaneously from more than one transmitter of All India Radio will be deemed as one broadcast for the purpose of this clause.

(8) The Government further agrees that AIR will give credit to the film and the artist at the time of broadcasting of the Gramphone record or records of any songs covered by clause 4 of this agreement.

(9) Each of the parties hereto shall during the subsistance of this agreement, furnish to the other all such information as may be in its possession and which is circulated to enable the parties hereto to protect and defend their common interests. The Director General shall furnish to the producer the names of songs from particular films broadcast from the Stations at All India Radio every year and the number of times each song was broadcast.

(10) This agreement shall remain in force for a period of three years from the..14th..................day of..May..........(one thousand nine hundred and eighty..Ninety four...and shall continue thereafter until terminated as hereinafter provided. The Government shall be entitled to give the producer six months' notice in writing of its desire or intention to terminate this agreement and upon the expiry of such notice this agreement shall immediately terminate as between the Producer and the Government. The producer shall similarly be entitled to give the Government six months notice in writing of his desire or intention to terminate this agreement

(G.C.P.) Ya 194 (3,000—7-89)

and upon the expiry of such notice this agreement shall immediately terminate as between the Producer and the Government. The notice of termination herein provided for shall be deemed to have been duly given on behalf of the Government if given by the Director General or by any officer duly authorised by him in this behalf to the producer if addressed to to the Producer and posted under registered cover to the address given in the commencement of this agreement, unless the producer has duly notified any change in his address in which case the notice will be deemed to have been duly given by the producer to the Government if addressed to the Director General posted under registered cover to the Director General, All India Radio, New Delhi.

(11) The producer shall furnish if he has not already done so, direct and simultaneously to each of the respective stations and to the Director General :—

(*a*) list showing the names of all the film produced by the Producer.

(*b*) the full texts of the songs used in each of the films.

(*c*) information in respect of each of the songs referred to in (*b*) above, showing whether it has been recorded, if so by which gramophone company, and what number also whether the manufactures' rights are vested in (or have been acquired by) the respective Producer. A statement as aforesaid that the manufactures' rights are so vested will operate as a warranty and the provisions of clauses 5 and 6 aforesaid will *mutatis mutandis* apply.

(12) In the case of each film produced subsequent to the execution of this agreement, the producer shall furnish information under (*a*), (*b*) and (*c*) above in respect of the said film not later than one month of the date of release of the said film to the public.

(13) Subject as hereinbefore otherwise provided all notices to be given and all actions to be taken on behalf of the Government and all rights exercised on behalf of the Government shall be by the Director General, All India Radio or any Officer of All India Radio authorised by the Director General, All India Radio, in this connection.

(14) Any question or dispute arising between the Government on the one hand and the Producer on the other as to the construction or operation of this agreement or the respective rights and liabilities of the parties hereunder or in any way relating to or arising out of these presents or touching the subject matter thereof shall be referred to the arbitration of a single arbitrator to be appointed by the consent of the parties hereto and the provisions the Arbitration Act, 1940 or any statutory modification or re-enactment thereof shall apply to such arbitration.

IN WITNESS whereof the President of India has caused on his behalf to set his hand hereunto and the Producer has duly executed these presents the day and the year first above written.

Signed by Shri N.S. KRISHNAMURTY ....
for and on behalf of the President of India in the Presence of
Kirtida S. Mehta
Smt. K.S. Mehta
Programme Executive
All India Radio, Bombay.

STATION DIRECTOR,
ALL INDIA RADIO, BOMBAY.
for and on behalf of the President of India.

Signed by the Producer in the Presence of
Shri/Smt. DEVI DATT SHARMA ....

Signature of Witness
Address of Witness : (DEVI DATT SHARMA)

[Rubber stamp/Seal of the Producer]

Signature
Name in Block Capitals : DR. SUSHRUT ALMAST

BHAVANI ... SERVICE
24/138, Housing Board Colony,
... (East),
BOMBAY - 400066.

Address of the Producer :
1. Office : 9 - SHANTI BHUVAN
CHAPEL LANE, SANTACRUZ (WEST)
BOMBAY - 400054.

2. ~~Residence~~ REGD. OFFICE : C-39,
EAST OF KAILASH,
NEW-DELHI - 110065

नवनिर्मित फिल्म 'निर्णायक' का आडियो केसेट वास्तव में संगीत में एक नया उन्माद पैदा करने में समर्थ है। श्रोताओं का एक बड़ा वर्ग इसे काफी सराहेगा, इसकी पूरी उम्मीद है।

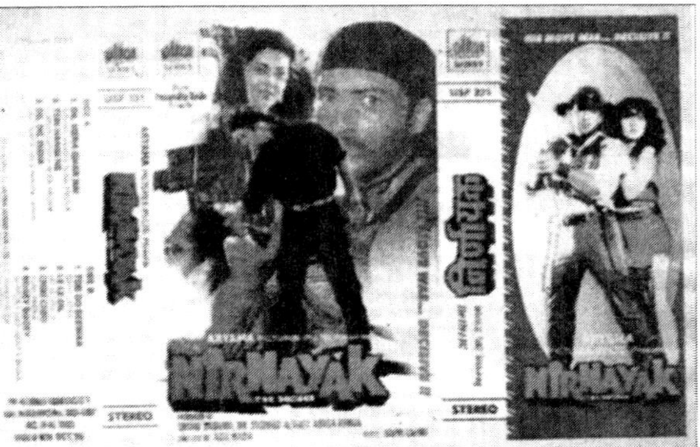

'निर्णायक' का ऑडियो कैसेट

[illegible]

Chamber of Motion Picture Producers

"IMPPA HOUSE", Dr. Ambedkar Road, Bandra (West), Bombay-400 050.

(MUSIC BUREAU) Phone : 640 63 44 / 640 63 45 / 640 07 67 / 640 60 97

№ 103646

Recording Date 14/9/92 Theatre [illegible]

Time [illegible] Take/B/G: [illegible]

Music Director Bappi Lahiri Artist

Name & Address of the Production [illegible] Name of the Inspector [illegible]

No.	NAME	Group	Instrument	Take Money	Conveyance	Overtime	S. No.	NAME	Group	Instrument	Take Money	Conveyance	Overtime
1	Vincent		[illegible]	[illegible]	—	[illegible]	37	[illegible]		[illegible]	[illegible]		
2	[illegible]		[illegible]	[illegible]	—	[illegible]	38	[illegible]		[illegible]	[illegible]		
3	[illegible]		[illegible]	[illegible]	—	[illegible]	39	[illegible]			[illegible]		
4	[illegible]		[illegible]	[illegible]	—	376	40	[illegible]		[illegible]	561	145	[illegible]
5	[illegible]		[illegible]	374	145	[illegible]	41	[illegible]		[illegible]	120	—	—
6	[illegible]		[illegible]	374	60	94	42	[illegible]		[illegible]	60	—	60
7	[illegible]		"	374	120	94	43	[illegible]		—	60	—	60
8	[illegible]		"	300	100	75							
9	[illegible]		"	300	60	—							
10	[illegible]		"	374	60	94							
11	[illegible]		"	374	250	94							
12	[illegible]		"	374	60	94							
13	[illegible]		"	267	120	67							
14	[illegible]		"	300	60	75							
15	[illegible]		"	267	60	67							
16	[illegible]		"	374	60	94							
17	[illegible]		"	374	120	94							
18	R. K. [illegible]		[illegible]	374	[illegible]	94							

Estd. 1952
Reg. No. 1396

Phone : 45 43 05

Cine Musicians' Association

UNDER POSTAL CERTIFICATE.

"Poonam" ★ Sitladevi Temple Road, ★ Mahim, ★ Bombay-400 016.

Ref.No.CMA/106/15/92. 22nd September,1992.

M/s. [illegible] Pic. Pvt. Ltd.
Santacruz (W).

BOMBAY:- 400 05[illegible]

Sub:- Overtime payment of Rs.[illegible]...
due to our members.

Dear Sir,

Hereby we regret to bring to your notice that the above mentioned sum of Rs.[illegible]. towards ....hours overtime is still due to our members of your Song/B.g.music recording held on.[illegible]. at [illegible]...studios, under Music Director Mr/Ms.[illegible]....

May we remind your goodself that as per the joint rule, you are required to pay the above amount within seven days from the date of recording or before the next recording, whichever is earlier. For your information, we quote below the joint rule regarding payments to our members, which state as:-

a) "the Producers' shall make Cash payment of Overtime charges to the Cine Musicians' on the Set, in respect of overtime involved for the first three hours Song recording, along with the Charges of normal shift of 4 hours of Song recording."

Song 4 **Bogi Bogi** Lyrics Maya Govind Singer Sharon Prabhakar Babul Supriyo

Song 5 **Chikky Chikky Bang Bang** Lyrics Maya Govind Voice Alka Yagnik

Song 6 **Dil Dil India** Lyrics Maya Govind Singer Udit Narayan Reema Lahiri

Out of these six songs, Dil Dil India was never picturized.

It was an item song and was planned to be picturized on Miss Universe Sushmita Sen and we had about 3 meetings with her but it did not work out.

So, the song remained without visuals.

Talking of songs, in those times, songs were such in which the story moved forward and this special feature was popularised by Sri Subhash Ghai.

Then there came the concept of **item songs**, which was just beginning to pick up and develop during the early 1990s.

Bappi Lahiri was very critical of the producers and directors of that time.

He used to say that producers and directors were not interested in either the lyrics or the composing of the music.

They would just call him to record a song on a situation and it was told on the phone that Bappi Da just make a Cabarete or similar kind of songs.

Producers and directors had stopped sitting with the music directors and lyric writers to discuss and write a song including brainstorming sessions for writing and directing and music direction of the song.

But it was different with us as we would sit through every song from the lyric stage to the song recording stage.

I remember when we were to pen down the lyrics of song Teri Hansi ne, for three sittings, we could not set up the mood.

Nawab Arzoo was the lyric writer. One day when it was raining and it was very beautiful in Mumbai. I and Anil invited Nawab Arzoo to a restaurant to write the lyrics.

As we were just discussing, a child with his parents came in the restaurant and sat on the table and he started singing the song **Mera Dil Tha Akela from film Baazigar** whose lyrics were written by Nawab Arzoo.

Nawab Arzoo was so inspired and thrilled that within the next 15 minutes he had written the complete lyrics of **Teri Haseen Ne, which turned out to be my favourite number from the film.**

CHAPTER 6

Film Budget
Writer Director Producer

Writer, Director, Producer

Commercial filmmaking is all about the cost of making the film versus the returns.

Industry people used to quote Subhash Ghai, he says.

The writer is free to think anything.

He can visualize anything and put it on paper.

Say there is a chase scene.

The writer writes that 50 helicopters are chasing the hero.

Or when it comes to the director, he would quickly realize that 50 helicopters is not a practical situation and the scene can be shot with 10 helicopters itself.

But when the scene comes in front of the producer, he is very careful about the budget.

He has to be clear in mind what kind of budget he needs to complete the film compared to the returns he is expecting.

So, he suggests to the director that keeping in mind the budget, we should plan the scene in such a way that there is only one helicopter that is chasing the hero but we have multiple cameras to shoot the scene giving effect of multiple helicopters in the chase scene.

So, budget of a film is very, very critical.

Once you finalize the budget, it should not overshoot itself.

CHAPTER 7

Film Budget
Some Important Numbers

Some important numbers.

Let us talk about some important numbers which affect the budget.

This was the period when the films were shot on the cinematographic film, Kodak.

These days the films are shot on a digital system.

Talking of a film script, an A4 page amounts to only about one minute of the film.

So, a 120-page film script actually means a 120 minute or 2-hour film.

Nirnayak was approximately a 130 minutes film.

ESTIMATE BUDGET - SHOOTING

Date: ________ Location: ____________________ Scene No: ________

Shift: ____________________ Artists: ________

	HEAD	C/				
1.	Raw Stock: NS/N:	[illegible]				
2.	Camera/Nagra Hire/Taxi Hire: 2500 + 200	27[illegible]				
3.	Camera/Nagra Attendents:	11[illegible]				
4.	Lights/Tempo Hire/Fused Bulbs: 2500 + 300 + 550	33[illegible]				
5.	Lightmen/Electricians: 8+1+2 — 150x8 + 250 + 125x2	[illegible]				
6.	Cameraman-shooting/Lab correction: 2500 + 250 + 1500 + 25	42[illegible]				
7.	Cameraman Assistants:	137[illegible]				
8.	Crane/Tempo Hire/Staff: [illegible] + 150x4 + [illegible]	17[illegible]				
9.	Meter/Generator/Van-Hire/Staff/oil/Diesel:	27[illegible]				
10.	Location Hire/Staff/Other charges:	5[illegible]				
11.	Artists:	[illegible]				
12.	Artist Staff:	17[illegible]				
13.	Costume Hire:					
14.	Makeupman/Hairdresser/Assistants: 370 + 370 + 185 + 185	37[illegible]				
15.	Dressman/Laundary charges: 150 + 100	253				
16.	Sound Recordist/Boomman: 300 + 200	500	250			
17.	Catering/Taxi charges: 25x65 + 200	1825	625			
18.	Spot Boys: 150 x5	750				

1) LAB CHARGES
2) MUSIC
3) SCRIPT
4) SETS & LOCATIONS
5) CINEMATOGRAPHY
6) LIGHTS
7) MAKE-UP
8) COSTUME
9) PROPERTIES
10) SOUND
11) EDITING
12) DUBBING
13) OUT DOOR SHOOTING
14) CATERING
15) ACTION
16) CHOREOGRAPHY
17) PRODUCTION
18) CONVEYANCE & TRANSPORT
19) ARTISTS REMUNERATION
20) JR. ARTISTS REMUNERATION
21) DIRECTION
22) PUBLICITY

GRAND TOTAL

CREDIT

INVESTMENT/FINANCE REQUIRED

Cine Film:Negative (Raw Stock)

1 FEET = 16 Frames
1 SECOND = 24 Frames = 1 1/2 FEET
1 HOUR (60 x 60 x 1.5) = 5400 FEET
2 1/2 HOURS = (5400 x 2.5) 13500 FEET LENGTH EDITED= 44280 MT
Ratio 3:1 = 40500 FEET LENGTH EXPOSED = 132840 MT.
Ratio 4:1 = 54000 FEET
1 ROLL = 1000 FEET
1 CAN = 400 FEET

1 METRE = 3.28 FEET
400 FEET = 122 METRE
1000 FEET = 305 METRE

1 REEL = 9 minutes
2 HR 24 MIN = 144 MIN = 16 REEL

Secondly, speaking of the cinematographic film, the raw stock which is used to shoot the film was a Kodak film and we used the stock to the film ratio of one is to two.

This means that for every two reels we shot, one was the final product.

But for some big producers this ratio would go up to 60 to one.

That is for every 60 reels that they shoot, one is the final product and they will shoot about six hours of the film and edit it to be 2 1/2 to 3 hours.

But on the other hand, **Mahesh Bhatt** kind of budget producers, used a raw stock ratio of final product ratio of four to one.

That is for every four reels shot one reel is the final product. So, for a film of about 16 reels, it would be about 64 reels which would be shot and 16 would be the final product.

So normally a film is about 14 to 16 reels and one single reel is 10 minute of film time, which comes down to 140 to 160 minutes of the entire film.

Thirdly, a shooting shift is about 8 hours and 1 1/2 shift is of 12 hours, so it would require roughly 60 to 80 shifts for a film.

A Budget film, Nirnayak was shot in 60 days with 75 shifts so one shift technically gives 1 1/2 to 2 minutes of the final film. That is, if we shoot for one day you get a final film of about 1 1/2 to 2 minutes in a budget film.

Another technique to shoot films in a very short period of time is to have two to three direction teams at different locations with different stars and it will reduce the cost and time of making the film.

Also, budgeting or films for commercial screening is very important as the returns on the film is directly related to the budget.

Film is classified as a hit if it has box office collections of twice the budget and a blockbuster If the box office collection are four times the budget.

It is a flop if the recovery at box office is up to 50% of the budget and if it is less than 50%, it is called a disaster.

The box office collections from the theatres are shared in roughly the following ratio.

Producer gets 40%, distributor get 30% and exhibitor theatre owners get 30%.

This is the box office.

Box office basically means the theatrical collections.
There are other releases like OTT or satellite or TV channels which is separate.

CHAPTER 8

Film Budget Set Costing and Song Picturization

Set Costing and Song Picturization

Sets are a regular feature of Bollywood film and in Nirnayak we had about three sets at different locations.

There was a set which was erected as a cottage in the film city and our art director was Madhu Kamle.

So, once we discussed the set which was to be erected and asked Madhu Kamle for the budget.

He said that this kind of set will cost about 10 lakhs of rupees.

Now we told him that 'look it is a set which will be used for merely 15-20 days and after that there is no use of it so it would be demolished.'

OUT LOCATIONS

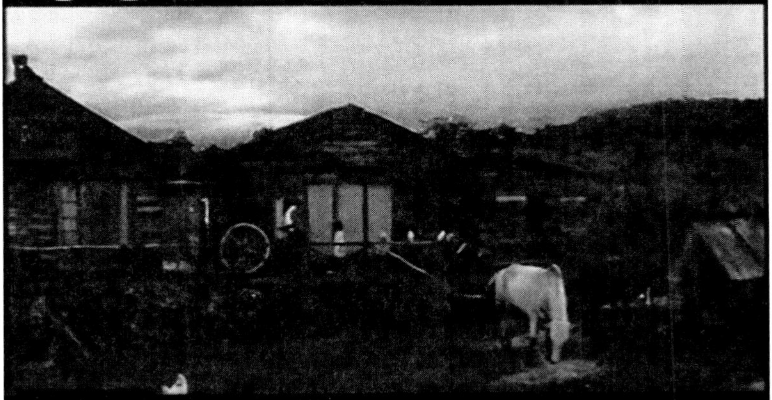

Film City Goregaon Mumbai

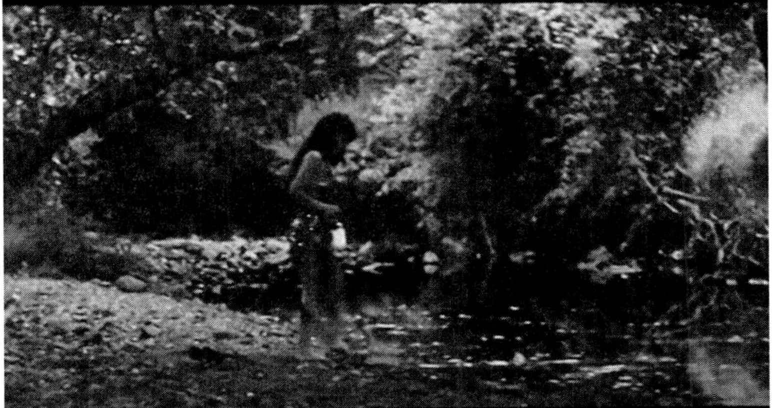

Borivali National Park

© 840 15 33

MAHARASHTRA FILM, STAGE & CULTURAL DEVELOPMENT CORPORATION LIMITED
(A GOVERNMENT OF MAHARASHTRA UNDERTAKING)
FILM CITY, Goregaon (East), Bombay - 400 065

Co. Code | F | C | TR. Code | 0 | 5 | 0 | 4 | **CALL FORM SHOOTING**

No. 21953

Date: 1 8 1 0 1 9 9 3

NAME OF PRODUCTION	SUB. CODE	TITLE OF FILM		
M/s Aaryama Pictures		Nirnayak		
		LOCATION: Kaliya Maidan	MARATHI / REGIONAL / DOC. VID. ETC.	/

Particulars	Quot.	Extra	Rate	Sub. Amount	Amount Rs.	Deduction Rs.
Location hire			2500/-	2500/-	2500/-	
Set Construction						
Set Standing						
Studio Lights						
10 Kw O/ H						
5 Kw O/ H						
2 Kw O/ H						
Baby / Baby Hologen						
Minibrute 6 / 8 Way						
~~Multi-way~~ Cable 13 days x			1 x 100		1300	
Hard /50 ft.						
Cutter Stand						
Elec Trolley						
Extn. Board 2 Nos (6-10- to 18-10) 13 days			13 x 2 x 5		130/-	
~~Pedestal Fan~~						
Camera Trolley						
Camera Stools						
Reflector Stand						
Reflector Ground						
Studio Property Hire					25/-	
Generator Hire Charges						
Crane Hire Charges			300/-		300/-	
Planks - Flats - Flower Pots						
Cables						
SUB. TOTAL						
~~Energy Charges~~ Power for 5 Lights					2275/-	
~~Water Charges~~ (13 days @ 35)						
Telephone Charges					100/-	
Recovery of Fused Bulbs						
Recovery of Damages						
Vehicle Charges						
Personnel Charges of Crane op.					50/-	
Tax 4 %					70	
TOTAL					6750/-	
DEDUCTIONS %					—	
TOTAL					6750/-	

Rupees (in words): Six thousand seven hundred fifty only

Payment only By Cash/D.D

Time in: 9.30 A.M.
Party's Signature: —
Time out: 6.00 P.M.
Party's Signature: Pradeep

Prepared by: [signature]

Checked by

Studio Manager

We don't have this kind of a budget.

He inquired what is the budget?

We told him that our budget is 2 lakhs.

We have to plan it in that way.

We don't need concrete structures.

Wherever possible, use paper, board, do whatever, but make it, the budget of the cottage set to 2 lakhs. So, he worked over it and from 10 lakhs he came down to about 3 lakhs.

Art Direction and set costing is a very important part of filmmaking. And if we have to work within a budget, everything has to be worked out accurately.

Everything has to be planned in such a way that we do not exceed the budget.

That is the way of making a controlled budget movie which ensures that you are able to recover the amount in making the film and if possible make it a hit, a super hit or a blockbuster film.

The second thing is about song Picturisation.

So, song picturisation can be at outdoor natural location where only the hero or the heroine is singing the song.

That doesn't cost too much and a song can be picturised in three to four or five shifts or maybe 3 days.

But in the case of a song which is on a on a set and when there are 60 dancers, it's a group dance song, then the budget increases manifolds and everyday paying 60 dancers - you can imagine the kind of budget involved in the song picturisation set cost.

So here you have to be very, very careful that the budget of the song picturization does not exceed with this kind of group songs.

I remember when we recorded our first song **Tod Do Dewar**, it was roughly a 6-minute song.

When we picturize a song, it's that we get only about 1 ½ minutes song per day.

So, a 6-minute song will need say a four-day shooting and costs include a set cost and the rent of the location.

Everything adds up to it and therefore we realized that this is going to have a burden on our song picturization budget.

So for the first time, I think in the history of Bollywood, we compressed the song.

We compress the song to about 4 minutes, 30 seconds.

And so instead of four days, we shot the song in three days, picturized the song in three days and saved additional expenses of one day. All costs - In terms of the shooting cost, in terms of the set cost, in terms of the rental and higher cost and in terms of the dancers cost.

And we could wrap it up in three days.

And then after that, whenever we were recording the song, we told Bappi Lahiri to ensure that the song does not exceed 4 minute or 4.5 minutes so that our picturization cost of the song is under control and within our budget.

Therefore, these are the two very important areas which determine the budget of a film, which is the **set erection cost and the song picturization cost.**

CHAPTER 9

Announce Your Next Film

We released Nirnayak on 26th December 1997 and 2nd January 1998 and the feedback from the various states was that the Nirnayak was doing a good business in every state.

But we were either not getting the actual box office sales collection reports of each and every theatre where the film got released from the distributors or they were giving us wrong reports and showing that there were less sales.

So we discussed this issue with the trade pundits at Bollywood that how to get the correct report. They suggested that there is only one way, that you announce your next film with a superstar.

Maybe you give some signing amount to the star actor and publish it in the trade magazines that you have signed a star actor.

Publicise in trade magazines that a Star has been signed for the next film to be launched soon after the success of Nirnayak.

And once your distributors read this in the various trade magazines, they will start giving you the correct box office sales at the end of every week, every individual theatre details including a share of profit.
They gave us an example that like in the manufacturing sector, if somebody manufacture shoes and he gives it to the distributors and they are in the market and somehow for some reason you decide not to manufacture shoes.

So, what they will do that, they will say that no, they will stop telling you the inventory position, they will stop telling you how much shoes have been sold.

They will stop corresponding with you.

And they know very well that now no new shoes will be produced and therefore you will lose the entire lot which you have produced because neither will you get the detail of inventory nor will you get your shoes back.

So, you have to now announce that you will be launching your next film soon with a superstar and then you will get the correct box office reports and also your share of profit.
Apparently, this is the way the industry works.

CHAPTER 10

As Kamal Sadanah Flops "Clash of Titans" Shapes up

Om Puri vs Amrish Puri takes shape.

By the time we had shot about 6 reels, Kamal Sadhana had many flop releases including Rock Dancer, Hum Sab Chor Hain, Kali Topi Lal Rumal and so the distributors were backing out and they were least interested in buying Nirnayak. I called my director Anil Wasia and had a meeting with him to brainstorm what should be done in such a situation.

We are stuck now and we have shot about 6 reels.

Significant money also has been put into the film. What to do?

And after long sessions of brainstorming, I told Anil to give me the contracts with Amrish Puri and Om Puri.

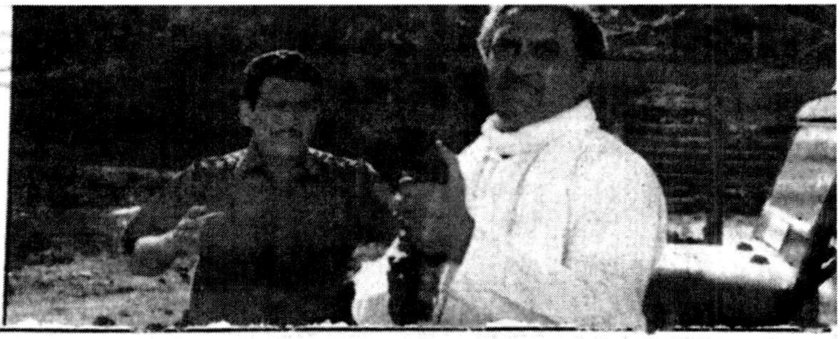

ओमपुरी और अमरीश पुरी की 'निर्णायक' टक्कर

कानपुर

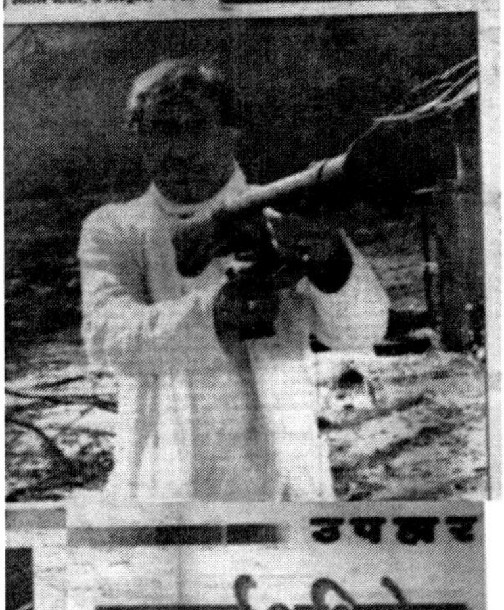

उपकार

सम्पूर्ण अभिनेता हैं अमरीश पुरी

असरदार अभिनय का नाम है

ओमपुरी

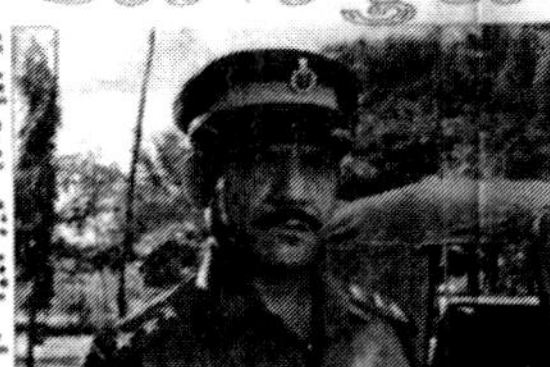

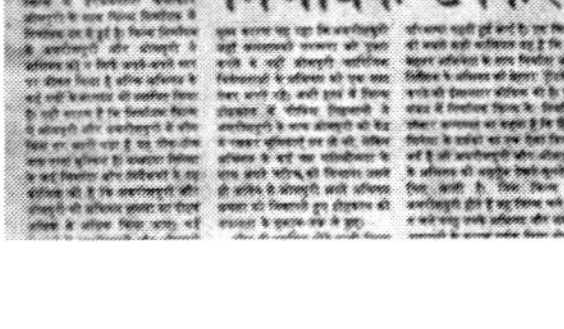

'निर्णायक' टक्कर

दो महारथियों की निर्णायक टक्कर

फिल्म निर्णायक में ओम पुरी और अमरीश पुरी एक-दूसरे के सामने हैं। देखना यह है कि कौन किसको मात देता है।

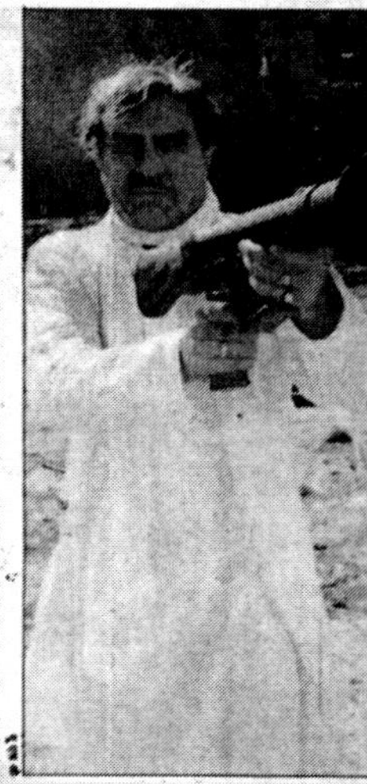

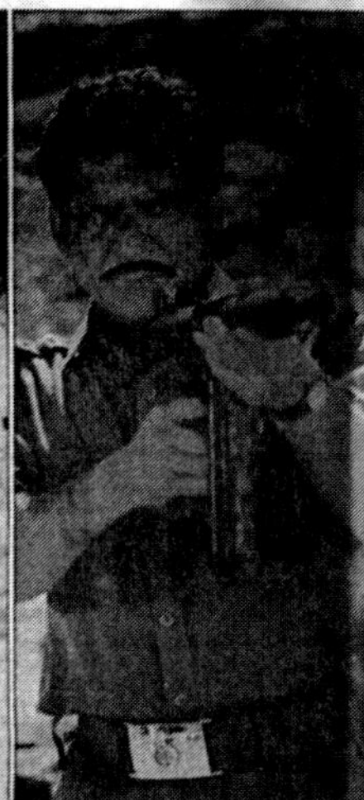

अमरीश और ओम पुरी का 'निर्णायक' मुकाबला

राजस्थान (अजमेर)

नायक-नायिका तो हर फिल्म में होते हैं लेकिन फिल्म को विविधता देते हैं खलनायक, खलनायिका तथा मुख्य रूप से चरित्र कलाकार। इन्हीं के प्रयासों से नायक या नायिका द्वारा निभायी जा रही मुख्य भूमिका में निखार आता है। अमरीशपुरी, अनुपम खेर, ओम पुरी, परेश रावल जैसे कलाकार जिस फिल्म में होते हैं, अभिनय की बदौलत कहानी की धारा अपनी तरफ बड़ी आसानी से मोड़ लेते हैं। फिर ऐसी स्थिति की तो बात ही क्या, जब इस स्तर के दो या तीन अभिनेता एक साथ किसी फिल्म में हों। ऐसा ही कुछ जल्द प्रदर्शित होने वाली अनिल कासिया द्वारा निर्देशित 'निर्णायक' में होने जा रहा है। 'निर्णायक' में अमरीश पुरी और ओम पुरी एक दूसरे के सामने होंगे। इन दो कलाकारों के अभिनय की टक्कर फिल्म का महत्वपूर्ण हिस्सा है।

अमरीश पुरी और ओम पुरी दोनों का साथ वर्षों पुराना है। आज दोनों ही हिन्दी सिनेमा के स्थापित नाम हैं, लेकिन ये तब भी साथ-साथ आए थे, जब उन्हें कोई जानता तक नहीं था। फिल्म थी 'आक्रोश' जिसमें अमरीश पुरी वकील बने थे और ओम पुरी खामोशी अख्तियार किए हुए कातिल। 'आक्रोश' के बाद अमरीश पुरी धीरे-धीरे प्रगति करते हुए हिन्दी सिनेमा के पहले नंबर के खलनायक बन गए। दूसरी तरफ ओम पुरी नायक, खलनायक बनने के बाद आज एक मंजे हुए चरित्र अभिनेता के रूप में स्थापित हैं और कोई किसी से कम नहीं है। 'निर्णायक' में अमरीश पुरी मुख्य खलनायक हैं, जबकि ओम पुरी ने पुलिस इंस्पेक्टर की भूमिका की है। अमरीश पुरी और ओम पुरी बिल्कुल ही अलग किस्म के अभिनेता हैं। दोनों में कई समानताएं भी हैं। उनके चेहरों पर फिल्म अभिनेता जैसा कुछ भी नहीं है। शुरु-शुरु में इन्हें देखकर यह सवाल मन में आता था कि इन्होंने फिल्मों में काम करने की बात क्यों सोची। थियेटर की पृष्ठभूमि से आए इन दोनों के अभिनय को प्रभाव देने में सबसे महत्वपूर्ण भूमिका इनकी आवाज की है। खुरदरे चेहरों वाले अभिनेताओं की आवाज किसी को भी सहमा देने की क्षमता रखती है। ये किस स्तर के अभिनेता हैं, इसके लिए अब किसी फिल्म का उदाहरण पेश किए जाने की तो और कोई आवश्यकता ही नहीं है। 'निर्णायक' के निर्माता-निर्देशक के अनुसार शायद ही किसी फिल्म में एक ही स्तर के दो अभिनेताओं के बीच इस तरह की टक्कर देखने को मिली होगी।

दो श्रेष्ठ अभिनेताओं के बीच होने वाला इस तरह का मुकाबला हमेशा से ही हिन्दी फ़िल्म दर्शकों को रिझाता रहा है। एक फिल्म याद आती है-'अंदाज', जिसमें दिलीप कुमार और राजकपूर ने साथ-साथ काम किया था। आज तक फिल्म विशेषज्ञ इस सवाल के जवाब पर एकमत नहीं हो पाए हैं कि दिलीप कुमार और राज कपूर में से बेहतर अभिनय किसने किया। 'मुगले आजम' में पृथ्वीराज कपूर और दिलीप कुमार की जोरदार टक्कर हुई थी। 'पैगाम' में दिलीप कुमार और राजकुमार में से आगे कौन निकला था, ये आज भी बहस का विषय है। वर्षों बाद दिलीप कुमार जब चरित्र अभिनेता बन गए, तभी उनका नाम इस तरह की कई टक्करों से जोड़ा गया। ये फिल्में थीं शक्ति (अमिताभ के साथ), संघर्ष (संजीव कुमार के साथ), कर्मा (नसीरूद्दीन शाह के साथ) वगैरह। कभी फिल्मों में खलनायक के रूप में प्राण का एकछत्र साम्राज्य हुआ करता था।

नई फिल्म

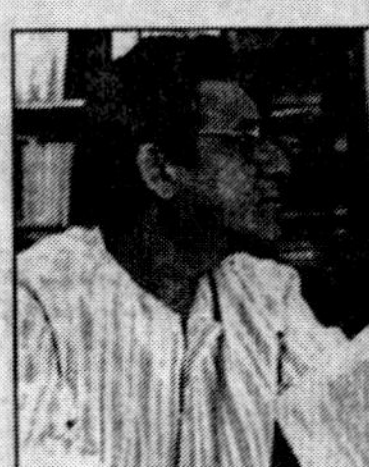

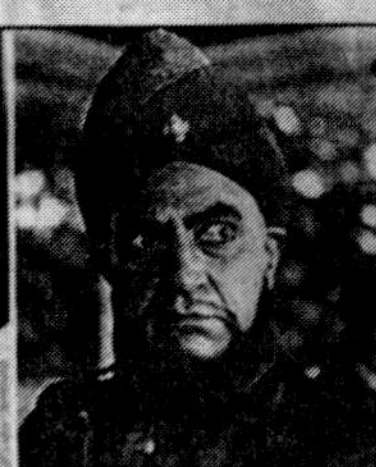

फिर शत्रुघ्न सिन्हा का आगमन हुआ, जिन्हें प्राण की टक्कर का विलेन माना गया। 'बुनियाद' में इन दोनों के मुकाबले की खूब चर्चा हुई और सिनेमा प्रेमियों ने अपनी-अपनी तरह से नतीजे भी निकाले। अमिताभ बच्चन, विनोद खन्ना, संजीव कुमार, शशि कपूर, ऋषि कपूर के साथ कई फिल्मों में प्राण कड़ी कांटेस्ट करते रहे। वह राजेश खन्ना के साथ भी 'आनंद' और 'नमक हराम' में आए। 'बॉबी' में प्राण और प्रेमनाथ के बीच हुआ मुकाबला उस समय सिनेमा देखने का शौकीन व्यक्ति क्या आज भी भूल पाया है? महत्वपूर्ण बात यह है कि जिस-जिस फिल्म में इस तरह के मुकाबले दिखाए गए, वह निश्चित रूप से हिट रही। 'निर्णायक' में और भी खास बातें हैं, लेकिन निस्संदेह सबसे अधिक चर्चित अमरीश पुरी और ओम पुरी टक्कर ही रहेगी, क्योंकि न सिर्फ इस फिल्म को रशेज देखने वाले, बल्कि खुद ये दोनों भी अपने अभिनय से पर्याप्त संतुष्ट हैं।

• शाश्वत

While doing research on Om Puri and Amrish Puri in trade magazines, I realized that both Amrish Puri and Om Puri, had rising career graphs and they were together coming in a film called Chachi 420 which was to be a comedy film by Kamal Hassan.

And we looked at other films, forthcoming films which were under production of Om Puri and Amrish Puri.

Therefore, I called for the contracts and luckily, I found that there were film contracts with no fixed number of working days.

When we sign contracts with actors, there are usually three kinds of contracts.

One is the per day contract, that is you call the actor every day, any number of days you want and then per day you have to pay a fixed amount you have to send to the actor.

The second is a number of days contract that you say that we will need you for 15 days or 20 days and the contract is based on the number of working days.

And the third is the open contract in which it's a film contract where there is no mention on the number of days you would be required to shoot.

And this type of contract we were able to sign with Om Puri and Amrish Puri because it was also the starting of their career and therefore, they had enough time and also they did not think that they should go for a number of days contract or a daily contract.

So luckily we ended up having a contract which was open and not a fixed days of acting. I called upon the writer, our film script writer and we discussed that as the career graphs of Om Puri and Amrish Puri are rising and their future looks promising we should increase their scenes in Nirnayak. On the other hand, as Kamal Sadanah has given so many flops his future doesn't appear to be promising. (Incidentally Nirnayak happened to be the last Kamal Sahanah film released in theatres.)

Let us make it Om Puri versus Amrish Puri, Clash of Titans "Puri vs Puri."

And this idea struck with the director and the writer.

I told the writer that you write about 5-6 scenes of direct clash between Om Puri and Amrish Puri and we planned to change the script so the film then can be marketed as Puri versus Puri – Clash of Titans.

While making a film and during the shooting of the film, a lot of things happen where you have to be open minded, where you have to be very creative, where you have to think how to handle the challenges of filmmaking and think out of the box.

And this turned out to be a good idea as ultimately it was our Om Puri versus Amrish Puri narrative, which actually helped us sell the film and make it successful worldwide.

Another thing which I realized was that why do commercial film makers go for two hero films.

Earlier while we were signing Om Puri, we had thought of Saif Ali Khan as an alternative for the same role whose career was just taking off and Kamal Sadanah and Saif Ali Khan could be shown as friends.

Om Puri was playing an Inspector role. With Kamal Sadanah and Saif Ali Khan an inspector as his friend it could be a good combination.

I realized that what happens is that when you start shooting a film **with two heroes**, by the time it takes about 18 months or two years to complete the film and release it, one of the heroes gives a series of flops and therefore he is out of the cinema goer's craze.

But maybe the other hero gives a series of hits and makes your film successful even before the release.

I realized later that at that time Saif Ali Khan was almost an unknown figure but then his film **Ye Dillagi** became a super hit the song **Yeh Dil Diwana Bole Ole Ole** becoming an overnight craze among the masses and **Saif Ali Khan becoming a star overnight.**

So some producers prefer a two hero film and because it takes about two years or more to complete the film and release it and one of the actors, one of the heroes fails to perform and gives a series of flops while the other one rises. **In such a situation you reduce the role and publicity presence of the flop hero and increase role of the hit hero.**

CHAPTER 11

Seven Years of Hard Struggle Never Gave Up

Went on floors in 1991 as Vyakul and released as Nirnayak in 1997-98.

Why did it take so long?

There were multiple factors.

First was that we started Nirnayak earlier as Vyakul with Ravi Behl as lead hero but as it didn't work out we replaced the entire acting team, the cast and we took Kamal Sadanah, Indrani Banerjee, Rakesh Bedi, Om Puri and Amrish Puri.
This took some time.

The second reason of course during the making of the film, Kamal Sadanah's films were not doing well and they were flopping at the box office and therefore distributors were hesitant to give further instalments and they wanted to be out of the film so we took the decision to make it an Om Puri versus Amrish Puri film.

Thirdly, we were short of funds having difficulty getting the funds to continue shooting the film.

Another major reason was that when we had signed Om Puri and Amrish Puri, they were relatively not busy. But as the film progressed, both of them were doing great roles and became very busy.

Their films were doing good at the box office and therefore it was very difficult to get their combined dates, it was difficult even getting their individual dates.

And all this added up for the delay and therefore it was a journey of lot of struggles during the seven years in the making.

I remember that on one occasion we could arrange money for just two-day shooting, one shift of eight hours costed at that time around ₹60,000.

So, we could arrange only about Rs 1,50,000.

I was in Delhi when I got a call from our Director Anil Wasia that we have got the dates from Amrish Puri.

You please join and manage the production part.

I didn't have any money.

It was so difficult arranging money and would you believe that I didn't even have money to buy the train tickets.

So what did I do?
I decided to board the train without the ticket and I took ₹10 notes, about 10-15 of them. And I took some place between the entry doors of the bogeys and the toilet. And I sat there without ticket. I didn't even had my clothes with me, just a shawl to cover myself up.

And every half an hour, or one hour the police team will come and I would just bribe them with ₹10.

Somehow, I happened to reach Andheri, Borivali.

And when the train stopped there, I deboarded the train and reached the office.

It was a one room flat in Lokhandwala, which in the day it would be the office and at night would be the bedroom.

I had no extra clothes with me so every day I used to wash my clothes at night and wore the same clothes in the morning when they were dried and in this way I continued for a week, with same clothes. What a struggle for an MBBS MD doctor!!

It was really tough, but because of the passion, because of the desire to see that the Nirnayak sees the light of the day, I continued.

This was one of the very difficult parts of the struggle while making the film Nirnayak.

Another incident I would like to share was a similar situation when I had to board a train without ticket to Bombay from Delhi. This time I talked to the TT that I have to reach Bombay by tomorrow but I don't have money to buy ticket and that I have to go for shooting of a film. The TT took me to his cabin and asked me to sit there. He assured me that he would take me to Bombay. It was Bombay Rajdhani. When the train started the TT came to me and offered my tea and dinner. He told me not to worry and that he would drop me safely to Bombay Central Railway Station.

He asked me do you know which place you are sitting? He told me that he used to take **Gulshan Kumar of T – Series** in his early struggling days when he was short of finances.

When we reached Bombay Central, he safely dropped me out at the exit.

CHAPTER 12

Never Forget the Cockroach

When you plan for the shooting, you must make a checklist of what all has to be done and what all items and artifacts are needed for the shooting.

This is the work of the production department.

The direction department makes a list of all the things which are to be done on the shooting day and that list is handed over to the production department to arrange those things.

Sometimes a small mistake, a small error may lead to the loss of lot of time, lot of money while shooting a film.

There was this scene in Nirnayak, a cottage scene with Kamal Sadanah, Indrani Banerjee and Rakesh Bedi.

And the scene required a cockroach which was included in the list of things to be done.

But somehow the production manager forgot to order the cockroaches.

The shooting location was a set erected in Film City Goregaon. And while the entire shooting crew and the actors and everybody was there, suddenly they realized that they forgot to order the cockroach.

The production manager then called the animal supplier to get the cockroach and the person who had to provide the cockroach said it is was not possible as it was daytime.

How do I get the cockroach now?

But we said it is an emergency, otherwise we will be losing the entire shift expenses.

He promised and ultimately got the cockroaches in the matchstick.

4-5 cockroach in the matchstick did come, did reach the shooting location, but by that time we had lost about half of the shift and which meant a loss of about Rs 30,000 because those days one shift of eight hours normally it costed about Rs 60,000.

All these small things do matter and they add up to the budget.

So we have to be very, very sure that an entire list, a checklist of all the things to be done and all the items required for the shooting of the day and the artifacts required and everything has to be on place on record and all the needs have been tick marked.

This will save a lot of time and money and also prevent disruption during the shooting.

CHAPTER 13

Animals World

I just told you the story of the cockroach.

Nirnayak was a film which was majorly short in jungles and had jungle adventure as a part of the story.

So it was natural that apart from cockroaches there was horses, monkeys, dogs even a snake, and a crocodile!!!

They were major animal characters in the film.

I have just narrated you the story of the cockroach.

It was tough for Rakesh Bedi, Kamal Sadhana and Indrani Banerjee to handle the cockroach.

It took some time for them to adapt to it.

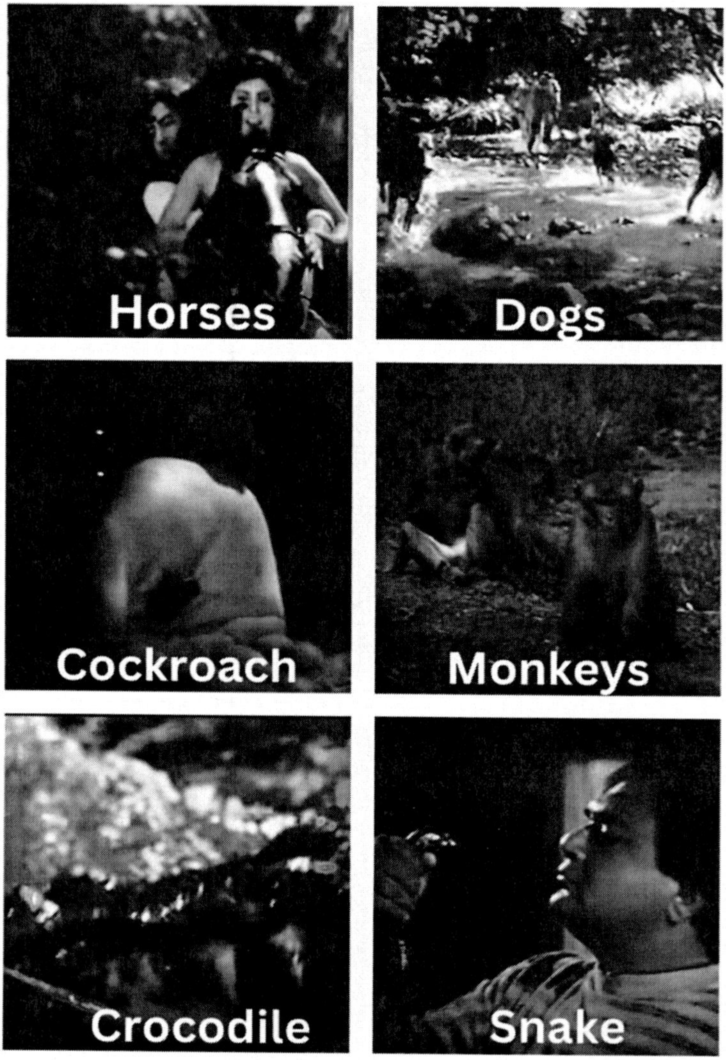

Similar was the case in the scene where there was a snake and in the scene, it was required that Rakesh Bedi catches hold of the snake and throws it out of the cottage window.

It took a lot of time to get the shot ok, because he was afraid of handling the snake.

Horses were easy.

Kamal and Rakesh Bedi were very comfortable on the horses while monkeys were a big problem because they would disrupt the set whenever they got a chance.

So, handling monkeys was again a tough job and the crocodile was naturally a dummy but if you watch the film you will realize that it looked so real.

It was animal world fun and those who love animals, who love the jungle adventures and the children, they really enjoyed these scenes with animals.

CHAPTER 14

God sends Ashok Verma

As Kamal Sadanah's films were flopping one after another and the distributors were wary of taking the film for the various Bollywood circuits, film circuits, territories.

We had already decided by the time that we will make it an Om Puri versus Amrish Puri film so that it becomes marketable and saleable.

But still distributors were not joining in and the finances were dwindling.

We didn't have money to shoot the film further and it was at this juncture that Ashok Verma, property dealer in Ashok Vihar Delhi joined us.

Somehow, he came to know that we were making the film Nirnayak and he came to me, my house and had a desire to be part of the project and join as a Co producer.

We discussed the project.

He had a very unique story to tell worth sharing

He had a desire to produce a Bollywood film and went to Mumbai to sign the writer, director, the technical team, the actors.

They zeroed on a particular film script, signed the writer, the director and gave them signing amounts. They gave the signing amount to some other technicians and actors. One of the actors which they selected was Danny.

So, when they went to Danny to sign him and narrated the script, Danny said that he is already doing the same script and it was a shock to Ashok Verma. It turned out that the writer of the script had sold the same script to two different people! Is there a way to avoid such fraud?

Now Ashok Verma was stuck up.

He had already invested about 15 lakhs in signing various technician, technical team and the actors and he didn't know what to do and therefore shelving the project he came back to Delhi.

But the desire to be a film producer was always there with Ashok Verma and therefore he met me.

We finalized the deal that Ashok Verma will be given the credit of the Co producer and the amount which was finalized to invest in project Nirnayak was sufficient to shoot another 10 days of the film which amounts to about 20 minutes of the film.

It was a real booster for our project because the very important Amrish Puri vs Om Puri sequences were being shot and therefore with God's grace, the film journey of Nirnayak continued.

CHAPTER 15

Freaky Rains Spoil the Show

It was a unique experience which showed that how you have to plan every moment and be prepared for all kinds of eventualities and still take action immediately as the situation demands.

We had a one-week schedule at Borivilli National Park and it was an 8:00 AM to 4:00 PM shift and we started shooting at 8:00 AM.

By 12 noon, clouds would appear and heavy rains started pouring, so the second-half of the shift shooting was not possible and we had to pack up.

This happened on 2 days and we lost money on half of the shift.

That is about 60,000 loss for two days.

Then I discussed these happenings with director Anil Wasia and we discussed the possible options and precautions we could take.

I suggested that we have got two options.

One is that we assume that this is going to happen again and again.

So, we have the shift timings from 2:00 PM to 10:00 PM and have some scenes which are to be shot in day and some scenes we plan for the night shooting.

The other option I suggested was that we do the outdoor shooting and we plan some indoor scenes also so that if it rains, we shift inside the set and we shoot some inside scenes, indoor scenes and when the rain stops then we can come out again and resume our outdoor Borivali National Park shooting.

So, from the third day onwards we applied this strategy and to our surprise It rained exactly from 12 noon to 2:00 PM on all seven days.

But since we were prepared from the third day onwards, whenever the rain started, we shifted indoors, did the indoor shooting and 2-3 days we worked in such a way.

We had a 2:00 PM to 10:00 PM shift, 8-hour shift and by the time we started shooting the rains were over and we could successfully shoot on all the rest of five days.

This is a classic example how freaky things can happen and one has to be prepared for plan B.

The rains were from 12 noon to 2:00 PM, all seven days, and we planned for it except for the first two days where we lost about half shift every day, but then later on we got control over the situation.

We did not waste a single moment after that and we shot the scenes as planned.

CHAPTER 16

In Film Advertising
Force 10

Liberty Shoes - Force 10.

When things start moving straight in the right direction, they start moving in your favour and when there is obstructions, the also come in a series, one after another.

Once Ashok Verma joined us as a Co producer, things really started moving very fast. We were looking for some brand for in film advertising to get some extra revenue and money to make the film.

And through a close relative of mine, I came to know that Liberty Shoes was planning to launch a new product, shoes by the name of Force 10.

ARYAMA
PICTURES PVT. LTD.
9, Shanti Bhuvan, Chapel Lane,
Santacruz (W), Bombay -400054.
Tel.: 6491802.

PROPOSAL

Sub: Advertisement of your product/services in our Feature Film Titled "NIRNAYAK" (THE DECIDER)

Dear Sir,

We are giving a little write up on our feature film and how it can be useful in promoting your product/services.

Star cast :

Kamal Sadanah & Indrani Banerjee are playing the lead roles.
The film also stars Amrish Puri & Om Puri in pivotal roles.
Shatrughan Sinha gives a special appearance.
Other co-stars include Johny Lever, Rakesh Bedi, Goga Kapoor, Tinu Anand, Anuradha Patel, Beena, Shammi, Yunus Perwaiz, Javed Khan, Tom Alter, Shiva, Siddharth, Jaya Mathur & Birbal.

Technicians/Other Credits :

Written & Directed by Anil Wasia, Dialogues & Screenplay by Anando Roy, the film boasts of some of the best technicians in the Bombay film industry today. It has music by Bappi Lahari, Lyrics by Indiveer/Nawab Arzoo, cinematography by Ishwar Bidri, Action by Mahinder Verma, sound by Akhilesh Acharya and choreography by B.Tharun Kumar/Nimesh.

Script/Story-Line :

The film is fast paced. The first half of the film is romantic and carries all excitement of adventures encountered in the jungle combined with pleasures of beautiful scenic locales. The second half is action oriented taking place in Bombay metropolis as the hero searches for the murderers of his family, kidnaper of his sister and fate of his heart throb.

Expected completion/release :

Three songs have already been recorded and six reels have been shot. The film is being shot continuously. We plan to release the audio by February/March '94 and the film in May '94.

As we know all the big companies are best utilising the feature film as the medium for publicity/promotion of their product/services. We intend to picturise scenes/songs in which your product/services through our film will help immensely in promoting the product/services.

Thanking You

Your sincerely,

(DR. [illegible])

Regd. Off.: C-39, East Of Kailash, New Delhi - 110065, Ph.: 634455
[illegible] Lower Circular Road, Calcutta - 700017. Ph.: 473240

7. The film will also carry **Theme music** whereever possible which will be supplied by us.

8. We shall be allowed to use the footage of the film where ever necessary for our advertising requirements or for other purposes and the same will be provided to us free of cost as and when demanded. No copy right whatsoever will be applicable on such footage.

9. No royalty or anyother fees or charges will be paid by us to any actor of the film for using the above footage.

10. Substantial amouunt will be spent for advertising the film through various medias and the due coverage / advertising mileage will be given to us.

11. Trailer of the film will run on Zee TV and other channels in which substantial indirect publicity would be provided to us by using the footage which carries our advertising message.

12. There will be no other major sponsor in this film and no other footwear brand in any manner **what** so ever will be allowed to be associated with the film.

13. Beside the above where ever required our consent will be taken by you for the success of the film as per mutual agreement.

14. The film will be released till 30 May'94.

Against the above a total cost of Rs 7,00,000-00 will be payable by us which includes the cost of Motorbike and Set for the songs. Out of the above amount Rs 2,00,000.00 is already paid to you vide cheque no 51330 dt 18-1-94 and Rs 2,50,000.00 will be paid at the time of picturisation of songs and balance amount of 2,50,000.00 immediately at the time of release of the film.

Kindly sign a copy of this letter as a token of your acceptance for our records.

We wish all the success to the film and look forward to fruitful business relationship with you.

Thanking you, We remain.

Sincerely yours

Adarsh Gupta.

LIBERTY
NEW DELHI

Liberty Enterprises
LIBERTY HOUSE, 4/42, PUNJABI BAGH,
NEW DELHI-110 026, (INDIA) PHONES: (011) 594371, 594214, 5417062
TELEX: (81) 31-79020 LIFO IN FAX: (91) 11-5455567, 5439647

11 FEB'94

ARYAMA PICTURES PVT. LTD.
C-39, EAST OF KAILASH
NEW DELHI-65

TEL: 634455/4622265

Dear Dr Almast,

Sub: Situational Advertising - Hindi Film Nirnayak produced by you.

This is with reference to our meeting held on 16 Jan'94 in our office at 4/42 Punjabi Bagh, New Delhi in which Mr Anil Hamirwasiya and Mr Rajiv Gupta were also present. As agreed we hereby confirm situational advertising in the Hindi Film NIRNAYAK which is being produced by you as per synopsis of the film submitted by you. Following is ag reed in this regard:

1. Throughout the film (as per the story) the Hero of the film will ride Sports Motorcycle & Helmet the layout & design of which will be submitted by us carrying our advertising message.

2. Whereever possible the camera will micro focus on the shoes carrying our brand.

3. Two main songs of the film to be picturised at the college function will be sponsored by us. The set of the same will be created as per design submitted by us at an approximate cost of Rs 4,50,000.00

4. The Hero of the film will be awarded LIBERTY TROPHY at the end of the song which will be supplied by us.

5. A motorcycle will also be awarded to the Hero of the film at the end of the above function along with Trophy and the same motorcycle will be used by the Hero as per para(1) above.

6. Besides the above whereever story permit due publicity and attention will be given to our brands.

H.O LIBERTY HOUSE, RAILWAY ROAD, P.O. BOX 103, KARNAL - 132 001 (INDIA)
PHONES: (0184) 21020/21102/45620 FAX: (0184) 21161 TELEX: 396201, 396202 LIFO IN

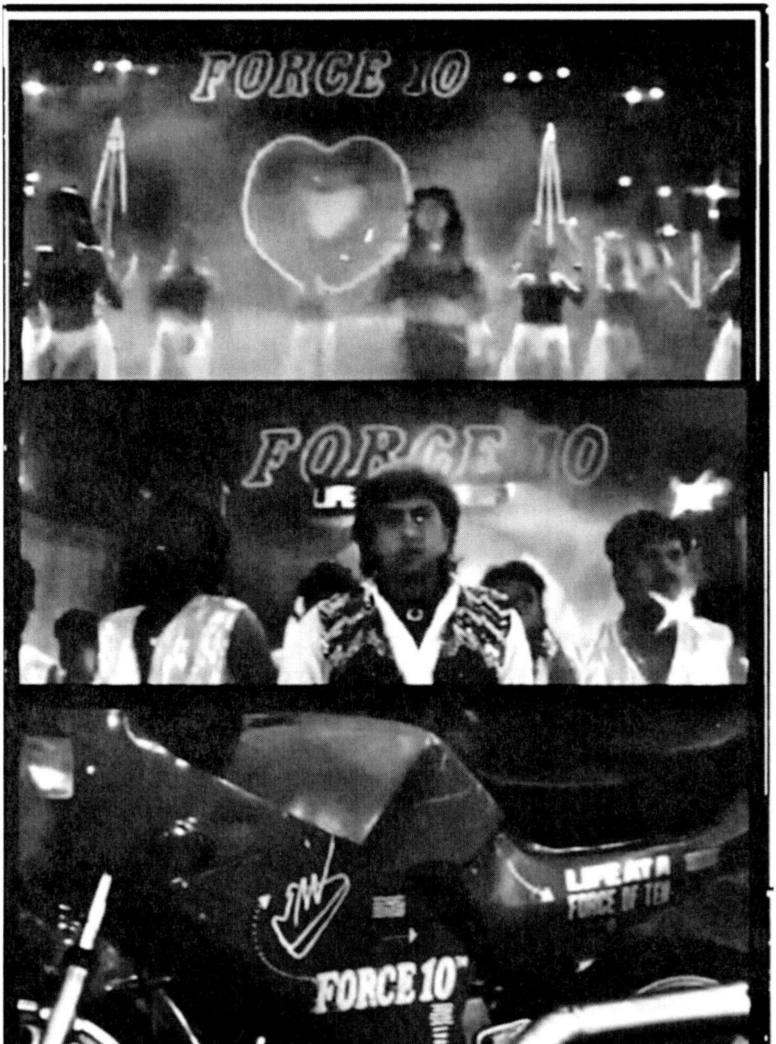
FORCE 10
FORCE 10
FORCE 10

We met Adarsh Gupta, director of Liberty Shoes and we discussed the plan that we would shoot 2 songs which were stage songs and we will erect the stage and put the neon signs and the Liberty Shoe Trophy in visually important locations of the sets. Also, there would be a motor-cycle with Force 10 written on it in with which the hero chaises the culprits.

Adarsh Gupta liked the concept.

The contract was signed and we were given sufficient funds as per the contract to erect the sets and shoot the two songs "Tod do Deevar" picturised on Kamal Sadanah and "Chiki Chiki Bang Bang" picturised on Indrani Banerjee.

Both were songs involving a significant amount of money as they were stage songs and there were 50-60 dancers and therefore a big stage had to be erected.

And the shooting also took about four days for each of the songs.

It covered up our cost of the two songs and we were able to move ahead with the project in film.

In film Advertising is a very important source of revenue for films and we were lucky that Adarsh Gupta of Liberty Shoes liked the project and invested in the two songs for advertising their product Force 10.

CHAPTER 17

Censor Board Blues

Getting Nirnayak censored from the Censor Board was a really challenging and harrowing experience.

Even after 32 cuts we were issued an A certificate.

We had to carry all the 16 reels to the Censor board about 8 to 9 times.

And after every viewing the censor board suggested something new frames to be cut, some scenes to be cut, some shots to be cut or some dialogues to be replaced and dubbed.

And it was really a very difficult and challenging experience for us.

There was a particular scene in which Kamal Sadanah kills the son of Amrish Puri, played by Neeraj Sharma. Kamal Sadanah ropes him up in the barbed wire and hangs his body from the fan above the bed of Amrish Puri.

High Court Delhi

FILM CENSOR REQUIREMENTS

Requirement	No:	Time	Cost
Shotwise Script (1)	8 copies	7 days	
Editing table (2)	4 shifts	32 hrs	
Complete synopsis (3)	8 copies		
Songs (4)	8 copies		
Credit Titles (5)	8 copies		
Booklets (6)	8 copies		
Application Fees (7)	100/-per 300 mtr(4587mtr)		1500/-
Cineworkers Welfare (8)			2000/-
Censor Certificate (9)	1	3 days	
Screening Theatre (10)	Gem/NFDC		2300/-
Submission of cuts (11)	Taxi		
VHS of OK film (12)	1		1200/-
IMPPA Certificate Publicity material (13)	1		700/-
Lab letter for Footage (14)	On application		
	After cuts		
English scripts (15)	5		
Script-writer renumeration (16)			15000/-

कांट-छांट और तबदीली की विशिष्टियां / Particulars of excisions and modifications :

[illegible]

	Length in [illegible]
Cut No.1 Reel No.1: Deleted the scene where Vikram [illegible] and kills the [illegible] [illegible] showing without showing the wounded [illegible]	
[illegible]	6.00
[illegible]	17.[illegible]
[illegible]	[illegible]
[illegible] Deleted the words [illegible] to the girl	
(Replaced with approved [illegible] Sound Only)	Sound Only
[illegible]	
[illegible] Deleted the following [illegible]	[illegible]
a) [illegible] of [illegible] of the couple	
(Replaced with approved visuals: [illegible])	4.00
b) girl [illegible] her thigh [illegible]	
(Replaced with approved visuals: [illegible])	5.[illegible]
c) girl lying on sofa in black dress	
(Replaced with approved visuals: [illegible] ft.)	[illegible]
d) Man running his hand over the girl's body	
(Replaced with approved visuals: [illegible])	[illegible]
e) [illegible] on the man's face [illegible] girl	
(Replaced with approved visuals: [illegible])	[illegible]
f) [illegible] with the short blue [illegible]	
(Replaced with [illegible])	[illegible]
a) Man kissing the girl on the [illegible]	[illegible]
(Replaced with approved visuals: [illegible] ft.)	
c) Girl lying on the [illegible] and moving her thighs	[illegible]
(Replaced with approved visuals: [illegible])	
d) Man kissing girl's body from down to top	7.[illegible]
(Replaced with approved visuals: [illegible])	
Cut No.[illegible] Reel No.[illegible]: Deleted the dialogue "[illegible]"	Sound Only
(Replaced with approved dialogue: Sound Only)	
Cut No.7 Reel No.VIII: Deleted the visuals of blood on the [illegible] and blood spurting from the driver's mouth.	[illegible]
Cut No.8 Reel No.[illegible]: Deleted the following visuals in the song "[illegible]"	
a) closeup of heaving bosom	[illegible]
(Replaced with approved visuals: [illegible])	
b) girl [illegible] and [illegible] her legs	[illegible]
(Replaced with approved visuals: [illegible])	
c) girl dancing with legs apart in blue dress	[illegible]
(Replaced with approved visuals: [illegible] ft.)	
d) closeups of pelvic area	[illegible]
(Replaced with approved visuals: [illegible])	
e) all visuals where short blue skirt [illegible]	[illegible]
(Replaced with approved visuals: [illegible])	
f) man [illegible] the girl all over	[illegible]
(Replaced with approved visuals: [illegible])	
Cut No.9 Reel No.IX: Deleted the visuals of the Vikram's friends smiling as the girl is being raped in the car	[illegible]
(Replaced with approved visuals: [illegible])	
Cut No.10 Reel No.XI: Deleted the visuals of blood spurting from the gun wound in the head and also the closeup of the dead man's bloody face	[illegible]
Cut No.11 Reel No.XII: Deleted the [illegible] of the flogging of the [illegible]	[illegible]
Cut No.12 Reel No.XII: Deleted the following visuals	
a) [illegible] face of the man falling on the car	[illegible]
b) blood spurting from the mouth and blood stained face	[illegible]
c) Retaining only two visuals of the hanging body [illegible] on [illegible] deleting all others.	[illegible]
(Length Retained: [illegible] ft.)	
Cut No.13 Reel No.XIII: Deleted the following dialogues	
a) [illegible]	Sound Only
(Replaced with approved dialogue: Sound Only)	
b) [illegible]	Sound Only
(Replaced with approved dialogue: Sound Only)	
c) [illegible]	Sound Only
(Replaced with approved dialogue: Sound Only)	
Cut No.[illegible] Reel No.[illegible]: a) Deleted the word "[illegible]"	Sound Only
(Replaced with approved word: Sound Only)	
b) Deleted the gory visuals of blood in the climax scene.	[illegible]
Total:	[illegible]

Total Deletions: [illegible]
Total Replacements: [illegible]
Total length of the Film: [illegible]

[illegible signature]

Chairman,
[illegible] September, [illegible]

[illegible signature] 24/9/97

Censor

(TO BE TYPED ON YOUR LETTER-HEAD)

Date:

The Secretary,
Publicity Screening Committee of Films,
'IMPPA House',
Dr Ambedkar Road,
Bandra (W),
BOMBAY-400 050.

Dear Sir,

Re: Approval of publicity - our film titled '________
Language - ________

We are forwarding herewith the following publicity and poster designs with a request to kindly get it approved and issue us a certificate to that effect for onward submission to the Central Board of Film Certification:

_____ 6 Sheet Poster/Banner Designs

_____ 3 Sheet Poster/Banner Designs

_____ 30"x40" size Poster/Booklet Designs

1(one) Photoset comprising of _____ Photographs

We are also sending herewith the requisite fee (i.e. Rs.700/- for feature films and Rs.100/- in case of Video films)

Thanking you,

Yours faithfully,
for

PROPRIETOR/PARTNER

I/We am/are member of ______
and our Membership No. is ____

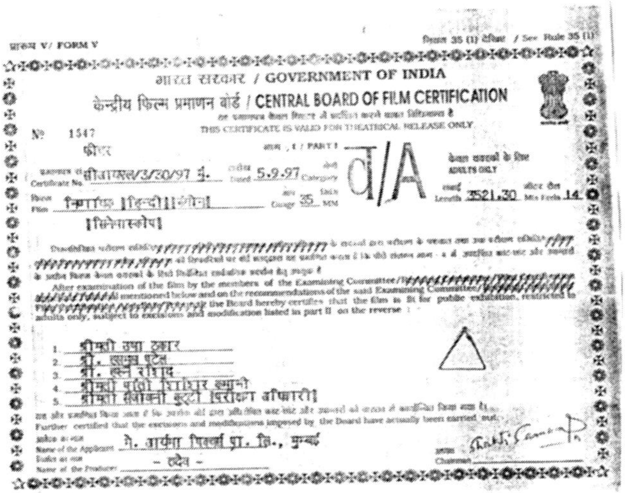

भारत सरकार / GOVERNMENT OF INDIA

केन्द्रीय फिल्म प्रमाणन बोर्ड / CENTRAL BOARD OF FILM CERTIFICATION

THIS CERTIFICATE IS VALID FOR THEATRICAL RELEASE ONLY

No 1547

A

ADULTS ONLY

After examination of the film by the members of the Examining Committee mentioned below and on the recommendations of the said Examining Committee the Board hereby certifies that the film is fit for public exhibition, restricted to adults only, subject to excisions and modification listed in part II on the reverse.

Further certified that the excisions and modifications imposed by the Board have actually been carried out.

Frames from this scene formed part of many scenes in the film.

There were about 18 shots of that particular scene and after cutting the shots as per the censor board, the final shots allowed came down to came down to just two shots.

Only two scenes or two shots were allowed and even after that we were given an A certificate.!!!

We requested the censor board to at least issue us an UA certificate, but it was denied. We then discussed the matter.

We thought that we would go up to the review committee in Delhi.

But then we were advised that two things can happen.

Either you get relief or maybe they add on some new cuts and still give an A Certificate.

So, it is better to release the film with an A certificate and not take any further risks.

Many completed films are lying unreleased, in boxes with zero value as they were not passed by the Censor Board.
A Juhi Chawala film was denied a censor certificate on account of "cruelty to animals." It never saw the light of the day.

During those visits to censor board, I also happened to meet Rajeev Rai, producer, Director of Film "Gupt" with Bobby Deol, Manisha Koirala and Kajol in the lead. Rajiv Rai told me that that he was also facing censor issues but more importantly one thing which he mentioned which every filmmaker and every film lover should know is the uncertainties of filmmaking.

In the 1st schedule of shooting of Gupt itself, Bobby Deol fell from the horse and got his bone fractured and it took about 3 months for him to revive and fit to resume shooting. During this period Kajol and Manisha Koirala became so busy that he could not get dates and particularly the combination dates of Bobby Deol, Manisha Koirala and Kajol and therefore his film Gupt took more than three years to get completed. Even big film maker like Rajiv Rai gets stuck with projects. Such are the uncertainties of film making.

So just to highlight the difficulties and the uncertainties which come while making a high budget commercial cinema and we have to be very careful of how to reduce these risk factors. I have shared some steps to prevent such mishaps in the chapter on Take Home Message.

CHAPTER 18

Fundamental to Success Legal Contracts

Out of 100 films launched by Bollywood outsiders film producers, only 5 films are actually completed, censored and released in the theatre. A strike rate of less than 5%!!!

Rest 95 are stuck up at various stages for various reasons.

6 Reel, 8 Reel, 10 Reel shot, not able to get a censor certificate or even after obtaining a censor certificate.

The reasons are innumerable.

Why films get stuck up at various stages?

It could be financial issues.

THE CINE ARTISTES' ASSOCIATION

(Registered under the Indian Trade Unions Act 1926)

Affiliated to the Federation of Western India Cine Employees Registered No. 3086

No.CAA/ /[illegible]/96 Date: 13.9.96.

M/s. Aryama Pictures,
Flat No.301, Satpuda .
New Link Road,
Adarsh Nagar,
Jogeshwari (W)Mumbai 60.

Re : Ms.Trishna Ghai VS. Aryama Pictures (P) Ltd., - Picture Nirnayak.

Dear Sirs,

Our member Ms. Trishna Ghai has handed to us her correspondence with you in the above matter.

It is observed that while in Confirmation letter dt. 17.4.94 you have mentioned her role as of 'LEAD ACTRESS' in your letter of 11.8.96 you say that you had engaged as on daily remuneration. You are requested to clarify thispoint, by by sending relevant papers to prove your point.

Thanking you,

Yours faithfully,
For THE CINE ARTISTES' ASSOCIATION

Rammohan

(Ram Mohan),
GENERAL SECRETARY.

B-5, GARIB HSG. SOCIETY, GULMOHAR CROSS ROAD No. 4, J. V. P. D. SCHEME,
JUHU, BOMBAY-400 049. Phone : 670 4568, 670 4569 ● TEL. & FAX : 628 4210

ARYAMA PICTURES PVT. LTD.,
H.O. : 143, Juhu Harshal,
J.V.P.D. Scheme,
Bombay - 400 049.
PHONE - 6491802

To,
Shri Bappi Lahiri
Juhu,
Bombay.

Date - 15-1-1992.

Dear Sir,

We are pleased to place on record that we have engaged you and that you have agreed to work as **Music Director** in one of our forthcoming film tentatively titled as VYAKUL.

The regular agreement, consisting of various terms and conditions, in respect of your services and remuneration, will be entered into at a later date.

Kindly sign the copy of this letter as a token of your acceptance of the engagement.

Thanking You.

Yours Faithfully
For **Aryama Pictures Private Limited**

(Anil Hamirwasia)
Director

I Confirm the above

(Bappi Lahiri)

Regd. Off. : C- 39, East of Kailash, New Delhi - 110065, Ph. 634435
Calcutta Off.: 6/3C, Lower Circular Road, Calutta-700017. Ph.:473246

ARYAMA PICTURES PVT. LTD.
H.O. : 143, Juhu Hanshil,
J.V.P.D. Scheme,
Bombay - 400 049.

Phone No. 649 18 02

To,

Dated : 17-2-1992

Shri Om Puri
Seven Bungalows,
BOMBAY.

Dear Sir,

We are pleased to place on record that we have engaged you and that you have agreed to work as Side Hero in one of our forthcoming film tentatively titled as VYAKUL being Produced and Directed by Shri Anil Hamirwasiya.

The regular agreement, consisting of various terms and conditions, in respect of your services and remuneration, will be decided mutually.

Kindly sign the copy of this letter as a token of your acceptance of the engagement.

Thanking You,

Yours Faithfully,
For Aryama Pitures Private Limited

(Anil Hamirwasiya)
Director

I Confirm the above.

(Om Puri)

Regd. Off. : C-39, East of Kailash, New Delhi - 110065, Ph. 634455
Calcutta Off. : 6/3C, Lower Circular Road, Calutta-700017, Ph. 473140

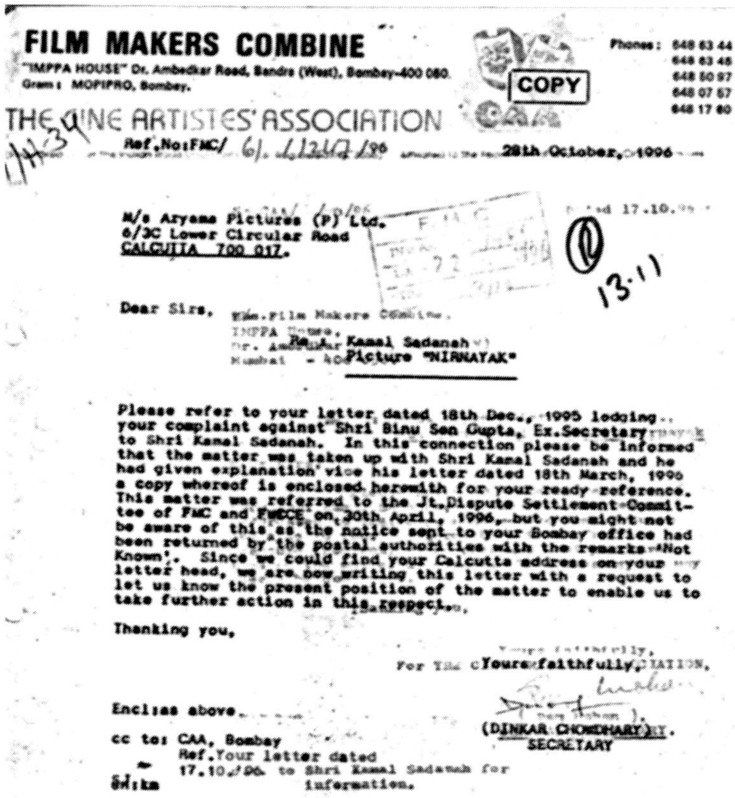

FILM MAKERS COMBINE
"IMPPA HOUSE" Dr. Ambedkar Road, Bandra (West), Bombay-400 050.
Gram: MOPIPRO, Bombay.

Phones: 648 63 44, 648 63 48, 648 50 97, 648 07 67, 648 17 80

COPY

THE CINE ARTISTES' ASSOCIATION

Ref.No:FMC/ 61/11212/96 — 28th October, 1996

M/s Aryama Pictures (P) Ltd.
6/3C Lower Circular Road
CALCUTTA 700 017.

Dear Sirs,

Re: Kamal Sadanah
Picture "NIRNAYAK"

Please refer to your letter dated 18th Dec., 1995 lodging your complaint against Shri Binu Sen Gupta, Ex.Secretary to Shri Kamal Sadanah. In this connection please be informed that the matter was taken up with Shri Kamal Sadanah and he had given explanation vide his letter dated 18th March, 1996 a copy whereof is enclosed herewith for your ready reference. This matter was referred to the Jt.Dispute Settlement Committee of FMC and FWICE on 30th April, 1996, but you might not be aware of this as the notice sent to your Bombay office had been returned by the postal authorities with the remarks 'Not Known'. Since we could find your Calcutta address on your letter head, we are now writing this letter with a request to let us know the present position of the matter to enable us to take further action in this respect.

Thanking you,

Yours faithfully,

(DINKAR CHOWDHARY)
SECRETARY

Encl: as above.

cc to: CAA, Bombay
Ref. Your letter dated 17.10.96 to Shri Kamal Sadanah for information.

SH:km

It could be legal issues between the producers and the Co producers, legal fights between the director of the producer, legal fight between the actors and the producers or any other technical issues.

There are numerous issues which can cause this kind of a problem. It is said in the film industry that the bread and butter of the film industry is earned by these kinds of outsiders, producers who spend money in making films but go back home with incomplete films or unreleased films with zero money recovery!!!

I am aware of the producers who completed 4 films but none could be released in theatres for some reason or the other.

Many Outsider Film producers are attracted to the glamour of the film industry and not able to complete and release the film in theatres due to various reasons.

As far as the big established production houses are concerned, they achieve good success rate of 70 to 80% releases, although their projects also get stuck up and get shelved.

The projects get shelved at various stages because of various reasons including that of market value of the film.

It doesn't justify that kind of a budget.

So legally one has to be very competent and have a very strong legal team starting from the making of the contracts with the actors, technicians, equipment suppliers and many other contracts, fighting the legal cases if and when they happen, including settling these disputes.

I think the number of contracts exceed more than 60 contracts from the various stakeholders including the cast, crew, distributors and others as I told you.

And, the chances of getting some kind of legal obstruction are also very high and therefore one has to be very strong in the legal department so that either disputes are avoided or if there are disputes they are settled very quickly, amicably.

We did have certain legal issues in the Nirnayak as well.

We fought more than 14-15 cases.

We had disputes with the distributors, equipment suppliers, even the artists one hires as crowd have very strong associations.

We had disputes with one of our heroines, Trishna, who complained to the Cine Artists Association that we promised her the second heroine role but was delegated to a small role. That we cut her role and made her look like just a dancer.

There were disputes with equipment, supplies, they were disputes with the other organizations also, and therefore I think one of the most important aspects for a producer in commercial filmmaking is to have a very strong and pre planned legal department.

CHAPTER 19

Thorough Professionals - Om Puri and Amrish Puri

During the making of Nirnayak, I realized that there is a difference in work approach between those who have come from stage and those who have not come from stage and directly having trained as an actor to join the profession of acting.

Om Puri and Amrish Puri have a long background of stage performances before they joined the film industry and I realized the difference in their thorough professionalism.

A week before their shooting day, they would ask for the script and the dialogues, the scenes which have to be shot.

They would call the director Anil Wasia, discuss with him the details of the scene and understand the mood of the scene and memorise their dialogues.

Even on the sets when the scenes were being picturized, they would have those dialogue papers in the hand and try to memorize the dialogues.

If there is a scene in which they are together, then on one side of the shooting area Om Puri will be practicing his dialogues and on the other side Amrish Puri**. A treat to watch**!!!
And the advantage of all this was that most of the time their first take would be OK.

Saving a lot of time and money.

Very rarely we needed a second take.

Another thing which I would like to mention here was that when we signed them and whatever the amount, we signed them for, in 1993 was nominal as they were relatively new in 1993.

But in 1997 when the film was ready for release, they had become some of the most important actors – stars in their own right.

In fact, Amrish Puri was always the main villain opposite the Khans and Kapoors and the big stars and Om Puri was a reputed supporting actor.

So, Both Om Puri and Amrish Puri were now charging very high fees by the time our film was ready to be released.

But when the film was complete and ready for release, we were short of funds and therefore we needed their help to waive off the money promised to them against Lab Letters.

Their professional fees against the lab letters which were issued to them.

That before release of the film or the print from the ad labs they would be paid such and such amount which was around say 40% of the total fees.

But looking at the situation that there was shortage of funds and film would be only released if their balance fees is waived off both of them were very cooperative.

What was more important was that the film was shot and was being released on Om Puri VS Amrish Puri theme. They could have asked for a raise in their fees but they stuck to their agreement.

They stuck to the contract which was signed and further more while Om Puri waived off his dues against lab letter, Amrish Puri did not ask for a rise as he was getting 10X more fees than he had signed Nirnayak for.

Another point I would like to mention here about both Amrish Puri and Om Puri is that now they were big stars, big actors, big celebrities of the film industry and they were doing big films with big producers and big directors. And we had problems with shooting as dates clashed with other films under progress.

Whenever we had to shoot schedule for Om Puri and /or Amrish Puri in solo or in certain scenes where they were together, we used to get a call from a big producer that they would like to get the dates of Om Puri and Amrish Puri.

We already were getting late because dates were assigned to us even three to four months later when we requested and therefore it was tough, but Om Puri and Amrish Puri stuck to their promise.

Whenever the dates were available, we had taken their dates.

They had blocked the dates for us and they never compromised on that or gave the dates to some senior well-known producers.

So, this is the quality of a professional who comes from the stage.

Those who have a training from some professionals acting schools are not that professional and even star kids are not professional.

Many of the star kids, never prepare themselves to get into the mood of the character that they are portraying.

They would just come to the sets and most of the times very late and then just ask for the dialogues, stand in front of the camera and shoot their scenes and you can see the difference of the performance of Om Puri, Amrish Puri, and those of vanshwadi and insiders.

The difference between professionalism of those who have a background of stage acting versus the others is obvious.

CHAPTER 20

As Nirnayak Hots Up

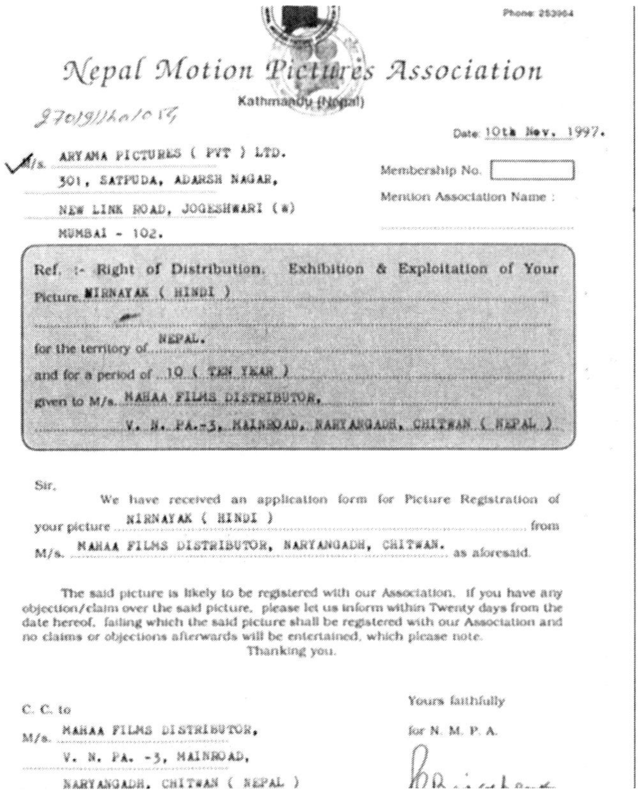

Phone: 253964

Nepal Motion Pictures Association

Kathmandu (Nepal)

Date: 10th Nov. 1997.

M/s. ARYAMA PICTURES (PVT) LTD.
301, SATPUDA, ADARSH NAGAR,
NEW LINK ROAD, JOGESHWARI (W)
MUMBAI - 102.

Membership No.

Mention Association Name :

Ref. :- Right of Distribution, Exhibition & Exploitation of Your Picture NIRNAYAK (HINDI)
for the territory of NEPAL.
and for a period of 10 (TEN YEAR)
given to M/s. MAHAA FILMS DISTRIBUTOR,
V. N. PA.-3, MAINROAD, NARYANGADH, CHITWAN (NEPAL)

Sir,

We have received an application form for Picture Registration of your picture NIRNAYAK (HINDI) from M/s. MAHAA FILMS DISTRIBUTOR, NARYANGADH, CHITWAN. as aforesaid.

The said picture is likely to be registered with our Association. If you have any objection/claim over the said picture, please let us inform within Twenty days from the date hereof, failing which the said picture shall be registered with our Association and no claims or objections afterwards will be entertained, which please note.

Thanking you.

C. C. to
M/s. MAHAA FILMS DISTRIBUTOR,
V. N. PA. -3, MAINROAD,
NARYANGADH, CHITWAN (NEPAL)

Yours faithfully
for N. M. P. A.

WEG
WORLDWIDE ENTERTAINMENT GROUP

WORLD DISTRIBUTORS OF INDIAN FILMS

8th, November, 1997.

To,
M/s. ARYAMA PICTURES (PVT) LTD,
252, Girnar Co-Op Housing Society,
New Link Road,
Oshiwara, Jogeshwari (W),
Mumbai 400-102.

Dear Sirs,

RE : Film "NIRNAYAK"

With reference to the above film, which you have assigned to us under agreement dated : 2nd November, 1993, we hereby provide the following clarifications :

1. Clause No : 2 (f) : Pakistan & Bangladesh are also excluded from the Entire World rights besides the countries already excluded namely India, Nepal, Bhutan, Sikkim & Nicobar Islands Only. Therefore, the rights assigned are for the territories of : Entire World rights i.e. Entire Overseas circuits excl. India, Nepal, Pakistan, Bangladesh, Bhutan, Sikkim & Nicobar Islands Only.

2. Clause No : 2 (j) : RIGHTS :
   a) Music as mentioned is in no way whatsoever connected with the Audio/ Music rights as commonly mentioned and known in the trade circle. It simply means the right to compile Video Tapes with the Songs of the Film, i.e. Music Video Compilation.
   b) Disc : as mentioned is in no way concerned with the C.D. Audio, whereas it means the right to produce Video Discs / Laser Discs / Digital Video Discs for the territories assigned to us.
   c) Satellite : We shall not sell/ negotiate/ offer the said film "NIRNAYAK" with any Satellite Company which operates in the INDIAN region, namely SONY T.V., ZEE T.V., ATN etc. We also confirm that we shall not sell Satellite to any Company whose footprints fall into INDIA. Furthermore, We do not have any objection to the Satellite screening of the said film (ON SONY T.V., ZEE T.V., ATN etc) bearing in mind that the footprints of these Satellite Channels also fall into the considerable parts of ASIA, of which some of these countries fall into the Overseas territory. The Producer shall broadcast / telecast the said film on Satellite in India as per Rules & regulations of IMPPA / FMC.

We hereby confirm the above,

Thanking you,

Yours faithfully,
for WORLDWIDE ENTERTAINMENT GROUP

KAVI JHAMANI - Proprietor

We also confirm the above,
for ARYAMA PICTURES P. LTD,

DR. SUSHRUT ALMAST - Director

8, Palm Crest, Main Avenue, Santacruz West, Bombay 400054, India
Phone: (9122) 6051011 • 6051842 • 6052933 • Fax: (9122) 6454554
E-mail: wegindia@hotmail.com

AUDIO PVT. LTD.

2-C, Thakkar Industrial Estate, N.M. Joshi Marg,
Near Sitaram Mill, Lower Parel (E) Bombay-400 011.
Phone: 3098458, 3078178, 3061554, 3065951
Fax: (91) 22-3061557

M/S. ARYAMA PICTURES (P) LTD., 19th July, 1996.
3, KRISHNA BHUVAN,
SECOND HASANABAD LANE,
SANTACRUZ (W),
BOMBAY - 400 054.

RE : AUDIO RIGHTS OF THE FILM, 'NIRNAYAK'.

Dear Sirs,

This has reference to the meeting your MR. BAGARIA & DR.SUSHRUT ALMAST had with the undersigned on the above subject.

As per the Agreement dated 21.06.1994 between M/S. RED CAT AUDIO & yourselves you have assigned to them audio rights of the film, 'NIRNAYAK' for the entire world on out right perpetual basis, and in turn M/S. RED CAT AUDIO have assigned the abovesaid rights to us with the same terms & conditions.

Looking to the present market condition it is mutually agreed between ourselves & yourselves to reduce the royalty amount by Rs. 3,60,000/- (Rs. Three Lacs Sixty Thousand Only) as compensation. Now the contracted price for the film, 'NIRNAYAK' will be Rs. 3,51,000/- (Rs. Three Lacs Fifty One Thousand Only) towards the assignment of above mentioned Aduio Rights. We have already paid you Rs. 3,51,000/- as under production amount which you now agree to treat as full & final payment for the Audio Rights of the film, 'NIRNAYAK'.

You further agree to deliver the dat master of complete songs, International track & complete sound track of the film,'NIRNAYAK' without any further payment or cost.

Thanking you,

Yours faithfully,
For ULTRA AUDIO PVT.LTD.,

(SUSHILKUMAR AGRAWAL)
MANAGING DIRECTOR.

We confirm the above,
ARYAMA PICTURES (P) LTD.,

21/08/96

Distributors started making a beeline with the news spreading that 70% of the shooting is complete and that the film is Om Puri versus Amrish Puri – A Clash of Titans.

Nirnayak became a hot property.

We gave ads in the all the trade magazines and in the distribution circles it was publicized widely and people got interested in the film Nirnayak, the Om Puri versus Amrish Puri clash of Titans.

Consequently, we were able to close the deals within the distribution circuits or the territories of Hindi films release which included the Nizam circuit, the East Punjab, then Bihar, Nepal, CP, Barar, Central India, Rajasthan circuit, Andhra circuit.

We also finalized our audio agreement with the Ultra Music and our overseas rights were also sold out, while the Indian theatre rights were all sold out on **minimum guarantee basis** which means whatever money they gave us even if the film does not perform, we don't have to return the money.

But if the film performs much better and once, they recover the money given and publicity expenses and other expenses, then whatever the extra profit is to be shared 50% each by both parties.

These were the agreements with our distribution territories.

Some distribution circuits including Nepal and music was then sold on outright basis, fixed total money.

We also sold the VCR rights, the cable TV rights and Indian satellite rights which ultimately later on we got back. We cancelled the TV rights and the satellite rights which instead of Ultra we later on released for five years on the Zee cinema.

So that was the effect of completing 70% of the shooting, and promoting the film as a Om Puri and Amrish Puri - Clash of Titans film.

And this did the trick as we were sitting pretty.

So now the issue was that to finish the movie as early as possible and release it, which we were planning to by December 1997.

CHAPTER 21

Tale Of Missed Opportunities

Nirnayak became a hot property after the trade magazines mentioned that 70% shooting is complete and it's an Om Puri versus Amrish Puri clash.

And as I told earlier, a majority of the territories were sold out but still the territory of the Delhi UP and Bombay circuits, which are considered the main and constitute about 40% of the entire Hindi film release circuits were on bargain.

We got handsome offer for minimum guarantee for both the Delhi UP and the Mumbai territory.

But somehow there was a difference of opinion among the Co producers and we lost both the opportunities.

The opinion of one of the Co producers was that we have to recover the money invested on the table.

And I explained that this is not a product like a shoe or a fan where you have a cost of making and you had a fixed profit of 15 - 20% and you sell the product in the market.

This is commercial cinema.

Here the investment to returns is very variable. From a no release where, one loses the entire investment, a disaster where one loses more than 50% of money invested, to a block buster where one earns 10x stakes and continues to earn money lifelong, anything can happen. The only prerequisite is that the film is released in theatres. Here a film may become a hot property even after many years of its release.

One could earn many times the investment or one could even not even recover the basic investment and even lose the entire investment.

So let us leave some space for the chance of the film becoming super hit and we receive the overflow.

You sell the movie on the minimum guarantee basis for 10 years to a distributor and once the film is released and the minimum guarantee and other publicity and his own expenses are recovered then whatever collections thereafter called as the overflow, is distributed between the distributor and the producers to the extent of 50% each.

That was the contract offered and therefore I told my Co producer, that we should leave some stakes for the possibility, that the movie is hit. At the moment we are getting distributors interest and if it dies down then somebody may not come and we will have to then release the films on our own.

And that is exactly what happened. By the time the Co producer realized what I was saying, the distributors for Delhi UP and Mumbai, the major territories backed out and ultimately, we had to release both the territories or Commission bases that we just recovered the print cost in both the Delhi UP and the Mumbai circuits.

But we didn't get any kind of overflow from the both the territories or any other territory.
One of the reasons could be that we were not getting the correct box office sales theatre wise from our distributors as well.

This is a very important issue that when there are more than one producers, the role of each has to be defined. A difference of opinion or dispute between the Co Producers may damage the product.

The space one has to take, is to be defined depending upon individual skills and capabilities.

And a lot of films never see the light of the day and stuck up at different stages of development because of the disputes between the partners and the Co producers of the film.

Another example was a case when we had to sign the overseas distribution rights and normally the trend in the industry at the time was that the distribution rights were given for 11 years.

When it came to the films overseas and music rights were sold on outright basis. **Somehow when our overseas distributor WEG – Worldwide Entertainment Group, drafted the contract, one of the Co producers who happened to sign it did not read the entire clauses and contents and he instead of 11 years signed the contract for 21 years. Every paragraph and point of contract is very important.**

Consequently, our overseas territory contract, which included the theatrical overseas release, the satellite rights, the TV rights for overseas mentioned a period of 21 years, we were stuck up for 21 years to resell the rights.

One has to be very, very careful when one signs the contracts, various kinds of contracts and a competent person or maybe a legal adviser is necessary to read through before the producer signs the contract.

This is very important part of filmmaking that if there are more than one partners, Co producers, as I have mentioned earlier, there has to be a great harmony among them and the role of each one has to be clearly defined, depending upon the skills of each.

CHAPTER 22

Still Photography Important

In Nirnayak our still photographer was **Anand Verma.**

3 Important areas where still photography is important.

Still photography means that for every day of shooting, every scene of shooting, the still photographer keeps on taking important stills of the scenes and the shots.

And the most important reasons for this is maintaining the continuity in future.

What happens is that when the scenes are being shot, later on at the editing table or even after the censor board recommendations, certain portions of the scenes have to be removed and new portions have to be inserted.

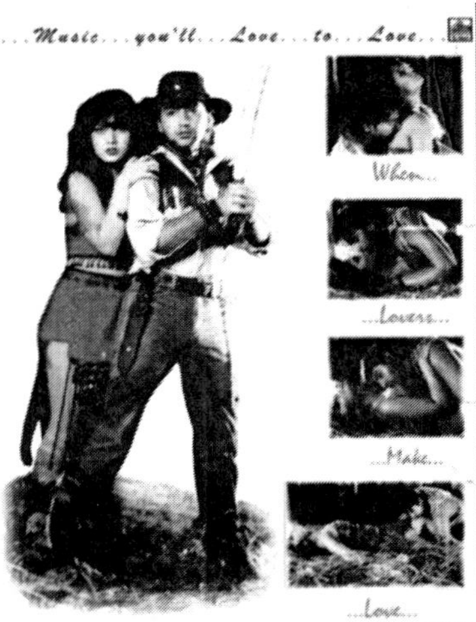
...Music...you'll...Love...to...Love...
When...
...Lovers...
...Make...
...Love...

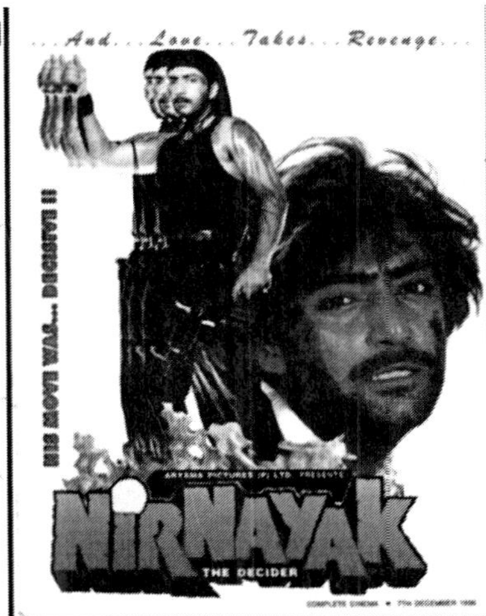
...And...Love...Takes...Revenge...
HIS MOVIE WAS... DECISIVE !!
ARYAMA PICTURES (P) LTD. PRESENTS
NIRNAYAK
THE DECIDER

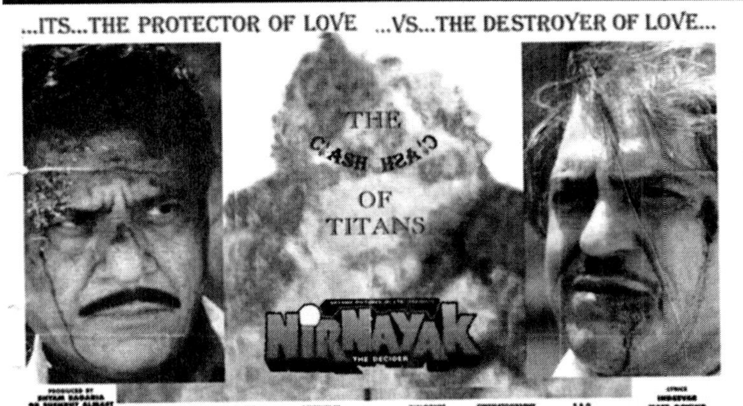
...ITS...THE PROTECTOR OF LOVE ...VS...THE DESTROYER OF LOVE...
THE CLASH OF TITANS
NIRNAYAK
THE DECIDER
For trade enquiries contact : ARYAMA PICTURES (P) LIMITED

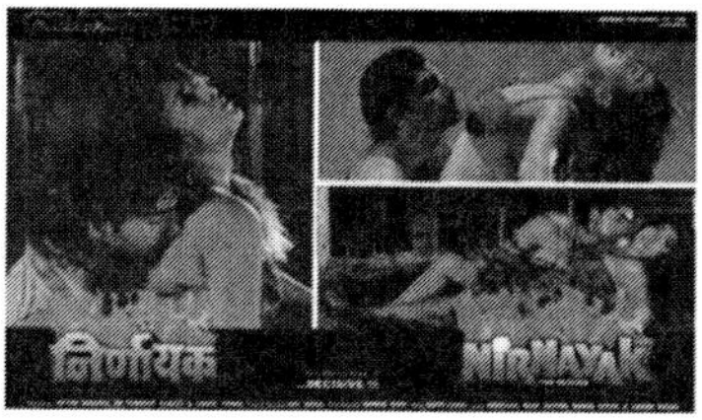

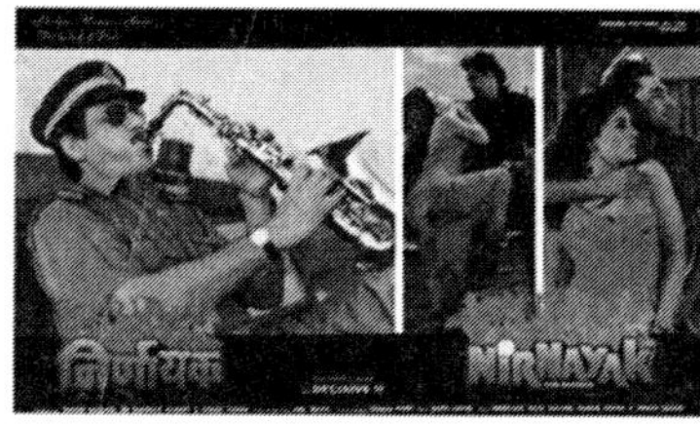

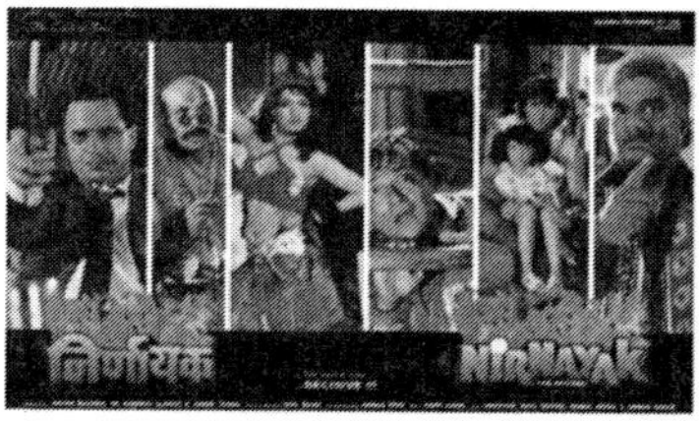

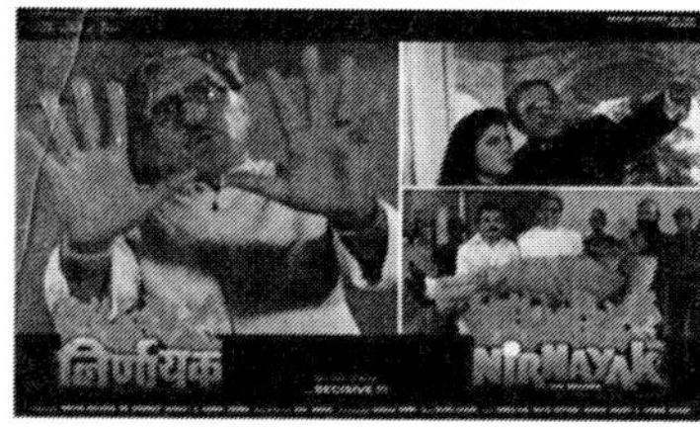

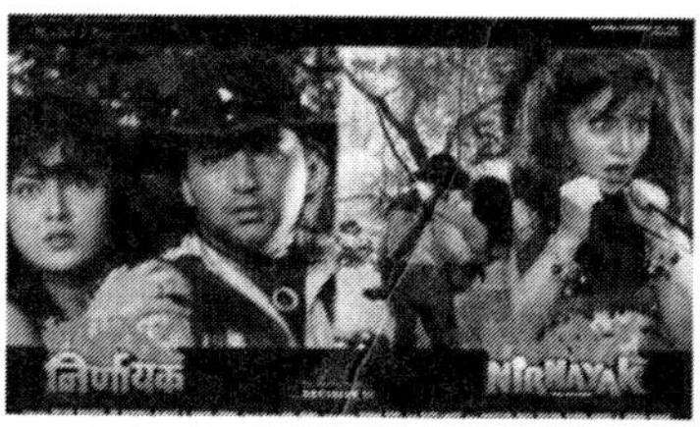

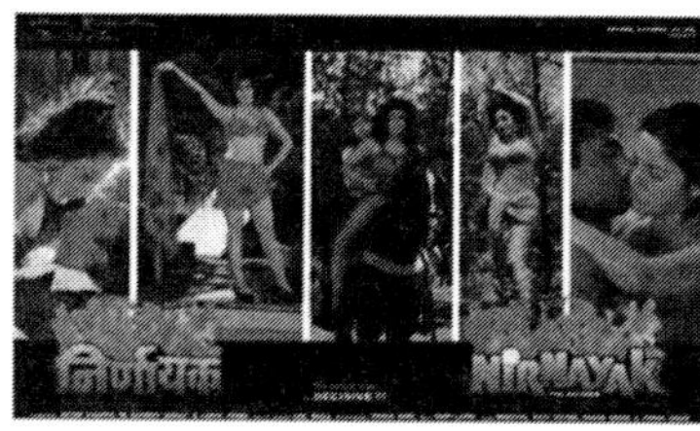

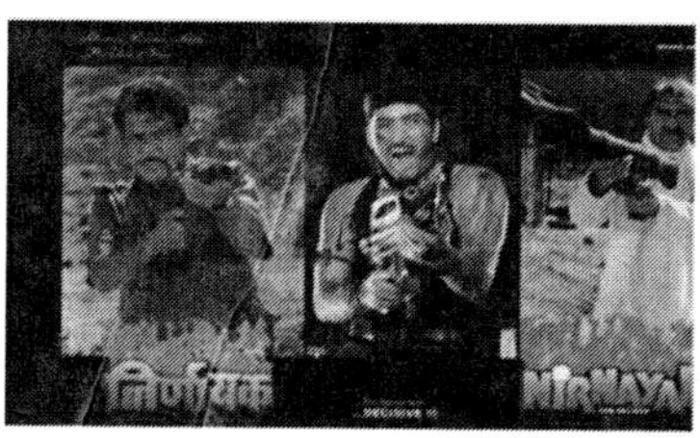

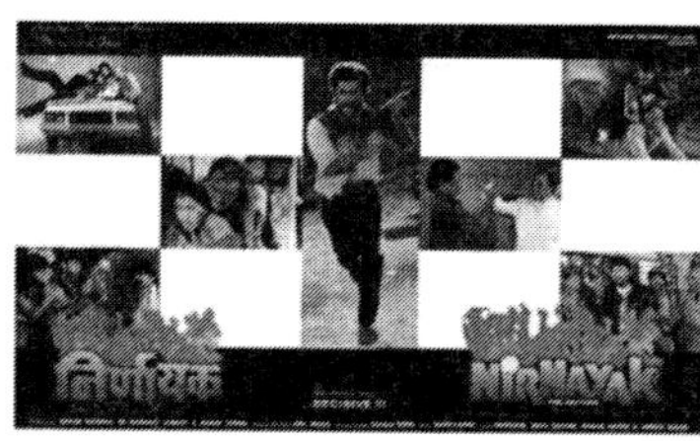

This is called **patchwork** and therefore during the patchwork of various scenes, we need to know what all actors were there in the scenes, what dress they were wearing, what was their relative position in the scenes regarding the artifacts and the front and background, what were the positions there so that there's no jerk and the continuity of the scene is maintained.

The other reason why we need these stills is that we **publish articles** in the various newspapers, the Hindi newspaper, the English newspapers and various other magazines.

We publish the articles and along with the articles we attach certain photographs.

So, if the still photography is good, we get good pictures to be shared on the print media and the newspapers, the magazines and wherever we want to share the articles.

The third important area of application is the **print publicity material** which includes the creating of **posters, banners**, photo sets etc.

The publicity material which is also delivered to the distributors along with the film include the **photo sets** which you will see that in the theatre, there are certain 7-8 photo sets which display the various important scenes stills. Photos are also needed in the booklets.

Booklets contain certain photographs and a brief about the story outline the lyrics, the words of the songs and the credits of the actors and the technical teams are there in the booklet.

Then there are **stickers** which are posted at different places.

There are also **bromide and slides** which are used to make certain important stills to be displayed in the cinema hall prior to the release.

Then there are banners, 3 sheeters, 6 sheeters, which are put up across at important places on the streets, on the roads and of course we have to give them to the censor department for prior approval.

Then they are also part of the so-called **quota publicity material** given to the distributors.

And there are certain **paid publicity materials** like big posters, which are called 3 sheeters and six sheeters.

And then we also have to give them the **trailers.**

So still photography holds a very important place in the entire filmmaking marketing and publicity process.

And in our case, we got the designs made in Bombay but we got them printed in Delhi at the Japan Art Press because of the cost difference we were able to save about 30 to 40%.

I think if I remember correctly, the cost of all this print material was about Rs 7 lakhs in Bombay and I got it printed at Japan Art press in around Rs 3 1/2 lakhs.

All the dispatches of the posters to various distributors and the of the various territories and film circuits was dispatched from Delhi only.

So still photography plays a very important role in commercial cinema though its value is many times undermined.

CHAPTER 23

Dubbing - Aastha For Aastha

Some coincidences really stun you.

When we had to dub Aastha's voice, Aastha played the child artist and she was busy in Delhi for her school exams.

So, we needed a girl's voice to dub her dialogues, and we zeroed on a girl in Bombay.

And coincidentally her name was also Aastha.

When we reached the dubbing studio in between the dubbing scenes, we were having a discussion.

Aastha had come with her mother for dubbing and I just happened to ask, as my habit is about Aastha, about the family and so I asked her where she belonged to.

They said that they were basically from Delhi.

I told her I also from Delhi.

And then I asked them which place in Delhi.

She said North Delhi Kamla Nagar.
I said I am also from Kamla Nagar.

And then I asked them which particular block.

She said E block.

So, I said I am also from the E block.

Then I asked which family in Kamla Nagar.
She said her husband's name was Vipin Chandan.

And I was awe stuck, because Vipin Chandan was my school friend from Birla Public School Pilani.

And then I inquired that is he the same Vipin Chandan?

They said yes and I asked Aastha what was her date of birth and she said 15th August 1985 and that happened to be the date of birth also of my daughter Aastha who was playing the role of the child artist in the movie and it was so surprising.

I said give me Vipin Chandan's number.

I called him.

We had been in school together but somehow after we left school we had lost contact.

It was the first time that I was talking to him since we left school. I told Vipin that I am Sushrut and like me he was really surprised and then we met at his home.

These are rare incidences, coincidences, and they really shake you as to how things happen in this world. Such a small world.

Also important to mention at this point because Indrani Banerjee had a Bengali accent, her voice was dubbed.

Well, I also got a chance for voice over. The very first scene of the horse race. The voice over artist who had to lend his voice for the horse race commentary failed to arrive at the dubbing studio and we were hard pressed to save time. So, we decided to try and record the commentary in my voice. And it came out perfect. In the process we saved both time and money!!!
Watch Nirnayak and share your opinion.

CHAPTER 24

Camera, Nagra, Lights

The three important, very important components of the shooting.

The cameraman or the cinematographer is a very important technician of the film because he is shooting the film and he is looking into every frame.

He knows exactly what all is visible in the frame and he is in continuous discussion with the director.

I remember that in certain important scenes our director Anil Wasia used to call our cameraman **Ishwar Bidri** at the office and they used to discuss how the shots are to be taken, how the scenes are to be made and details of the location and everything.

So that when they reach the location and they start shooting and it is in perfect harmony.

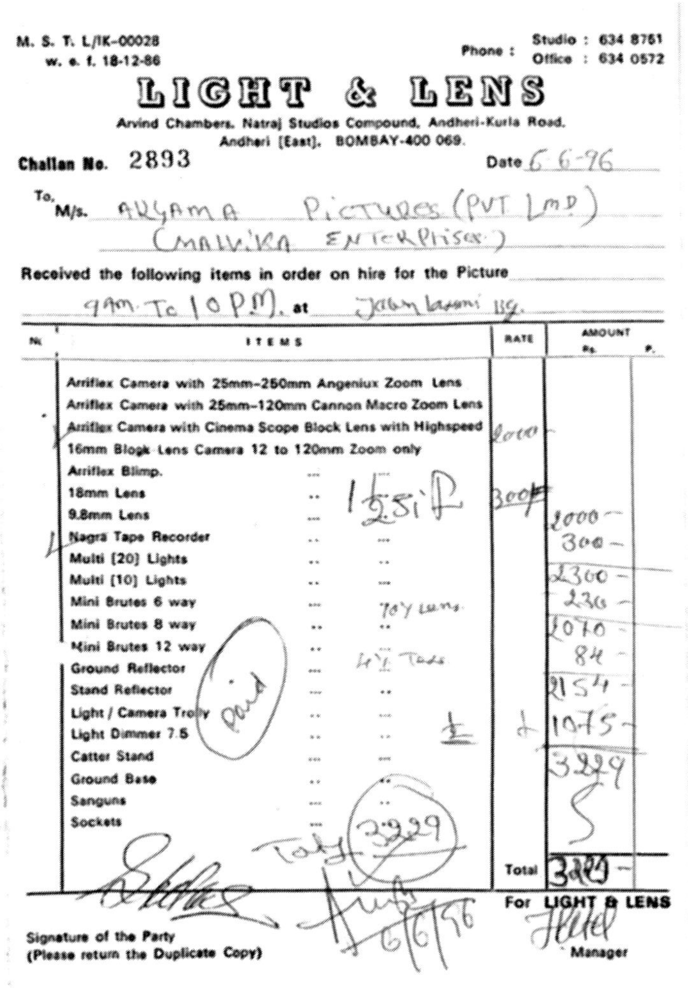

M. S. T. L/IK-00028
w. e. f. 18-12-86

Phone : Studio : 634 8751
Office : 634 0572

LIGHT & LENS

Arvind Chambers, Natraj Studios Compound, Andheri-Kurla Road, Andheri (East), BOMBAY-400 069.

Challan No. 2893 Date 6-6-96

To, M/s. ARYAMA PICTURES (PVT LMD) (MALLIKA ENTERPRISES)

Received the following items in order on hire for the Picture

9 AM To 10 PM. at

No.	ITEMS	RATE	AMOUNT Rs.	P.
	Arriflex Camera with 25mm–250mm Angeniux Zoom Lens			
	Arriflex Camera with 25mm–120mm Cannon Macro Zoom Lens			
	Arriflex Camera with Cinema Scope Block Lens with Highspeed	2000		
	16mm Block Lens Camera 12 to 120mm Zoom only			
	Arriflex Blimp.			
	18mm Lens	300		
	9.8mm Lens		2000	
	Nagra Tape Recorder		300	
	Multi (20) Lights			
	Multi (10) Lights		2300	
	Mini Brutes 6 way		230	
	Mini Brutes 8 way		2070	
	Mini Brutes 12 way		84	
	Ground Reflector			
	Stand Reflector		2154	
	Light / Camera Trolly		1075	
	Light Dimmer 7.5			
	Catter Stand		3229	
	Ground Base			
	Sanguns			
	Sockets			
		Total	3229	

Paid

Total 3229

6/6/96

Signature of the Party
(Please return the Duplicate Copy)

For LIGHT & LENS
Manager

There are a lot of examples where a person starts off as a cinematographer and ended up being the film director.

And I think the three most important technicians of filmmaking are the captain of the ship, the director, the cameraman and the third is the film editor.

These three have to be in a regular touch with each other.

The director has to be in a direct continuous discussion with the cinematographer and also the editor when the film is being edited.

On the table it is said that the second time the film is made is the actual time when it is being edited.

Nagra is the sound system and the sound technicians play very important role because when the dialogues have been delivered during the time of shooting the Nagra equipment and the sound equipment records all the dialogues and is very important because they are there at the time of dubbing to establish the relationship.

The sound system plays a big role when dubbing takes place and it also helps during lip sync.

The lip sync of the of the actor who is delivering or the person who is dubbing and delivering the dialogue along with the visual of the shot or the scene being run so that there is a perfect lip sync when the film is finally made.

The third is of course the lighting part.

Lighting is another very important component of filmmaking, often overlooked.

It makes the mood of the scene.

It helps in making the scene powerful and the lighting department in discussion with the director and the cameraman plans the lighting.

I remember a lot of films. I can quote here the Rajshree Productions where they would take 8 - 10 hours to light the sets or the location of the scene as per requirement and then the actual scene is shot for just 5 minutes or 10 minutes.

When the actual shooting takes place, it may just end up or deliver a two-minute to 3-minute film.

So lighting is very important.

You will see lot of films where lighting plays the main role in creating the mood of the film. Black with Amitabh Bachchan and Rani Mukherjee is one such example.

You will find that the equipment providers usually keep the lights, equipment, the different types of cameras, camera equipment's and also the sound system or the Nagra system.

CHAPTER 25

Stages of Film Production

Production normally is done in 3 stages, the pre-production phase, the production phase and the post production phase.

The pre-production phase includes the scripting and once you have the script then the financing part.

How you plan to finance the film and how do you plan to get the revenues and returns.

What are the various ways of earning money from the film and it also involves the location hunting as per the script like what are the locations in which you will be shooting the film.

It also involves the casting of the artist and finalising the technical crew.

It involves the decision of for which role which artist would be best, the role of a casting director.

The technicians, the technical team which includes the director, the cameraman or the cinematographer, dance directors, music directors, the sound recordist, the art director and all the other departments.

You finalize them and you enter into a contract with them.

So total number of contracts may be in the excess of 60.

Contracts with actors, technicians, equipment suppliers, financers, processing labs, contract with the distributors.

You could start getting some distributors based on your star value or the rating of directors.

Once you have the scripts you can pitch your script to a producer, saleable actor, saleable director or approach a producer after setting up a project after signing the main actors and technicians.

Normally they say professionally the maximum time you take one year, two year, three-year is in the pre-production stage and whence you have finalized everything.

And the production stage means exactly shooting should be finished start to go within 60 to 90 days.

Say suppose for a budget film of a 120 minute, we expect that one day of shooting will get our final finished product of about two minutes.

So, if you have a 60 to 70 day shooting days, then you shoot the entire film.

That is in case you are a budget director and not a director who keeps on shooting, gets a 6-hour film, then edit it to 2 1/2 to 3 hours film.
This is the production stage.

And sometimes to shorten the time in the production stage you have got two teams or three teams working at different locations so you save on time and on money.

The production stage also includes the patchwork, if any.

And post production includes the dubbing, the mixing, various print material, censor certificate, print publicity in various magazines, trade magazines, newspapers, satellite channels, TV channels, OTT channels.

So that is the post production and ultimately a date of release is finalized for release in theatres.

These are the three stages and they have to be planned very meticulously.

I think the most important part is the pre-production stage where you have to work towards defining fine budget details so that you do not overshoot the budget.

CHAPTER 26

The Business of Commercial Cinema

Business of Film Production is all about networking, networking and networking and reaching the right person at the right moment at the right place.

But along with that there are certain other things which budget Bollywood filmmaker should also understand.
A few options for a filmmaker.

Firstly, as a producer you need to understand that you are a commercial filmmaker.

It is all for the money.

You are here to make money out of filmmaking and therefore, even before writing the first word of the film script the entire plan of financing budgeting and source of revenues should be decided.

What are the various modalities you will get the returns from has to be worked out.

The film budget, how much will it cost and from where will you get the returns?

What are the various territories?

What are the various options?

You get money from the theatrical release.

You get money from release on Satellite Channels, OTT platforms.

You get money on selling the audio rights, you get money for selling the film on the TV channel, the satellite and all other options which are there with you.

These are the various options where you get the return and how much return you will get should be worked out on paper and everything matters.

For example, if you are signing an actor say you are signing Amitabh Bachchan and say for six crore he should deliver the value of at least 6 crores. Is he worth it? What is his crowd pull at the theatres? which is very important as what is the value of a star you are taking on the first weekend of release or the first week of release what he brings to the table.

How much crowd pull he generates in the theatre is very important.

The first week is the very important.

In fact, Friday, Saturday and Sunday i.e. the weekend is very important because by Monday the news has spread through social media about the film and the people then decide whether to watch or not to watch the movie.

So initial three days it is the star pull or the actor pull which gets the box office return.

But after that it is the content which pulls and the star value becomes secondary to the film.

And the content becomes the real hero.

So, whenever you sign an actor, you should know that what he's bringing on table for the film.

Beware of the hidden expenses of a star. Amitabh Bachchan may be charging 6 crores but he actually costs 12 crores as a battery of 15 people come with him handling his social media, costumes, make up boy, driver and more. We experienced these hidden expenses with Amrish Puri.

Now there are many approaches to filmmaking.

One of them is that you make a film and sell it to the OTT platform or a production house.

The second option is that the production house or the OTT platform gives you a story, gives you a script and a fixed budget and that you have to make a film in that budget.

The 3rd way of making a film is setting up a project.

You have a film script and you set up a project that this is the actor, these other technicians.

This is the time it is going to take these locations to set up the project.

A viable project which is then bought by a film studio and the film studio then makes the entire film and you get whatever your agreement or terms, either a fixed amount or a credit for a Co producer, whatever the terms and conditions.

But then what is very important is that somebody who is saleable or who has money or a production house has to be attracted to the script.

So, either your story or your script is liked or approved by a saleable star, or it is approved by a saleable director, or it is approved by an established production house.

Any of the three things has to be there with the script before you move ahead, because if the star likes the film script, then the setup is made immediately.

Finances will be arranged.

If a director, a saleable director, a big director likes the script, then again it becomes easy.

As you see most of the films released today are writer director films.

Because the person who is a writer, he directs the movie as well and he has got his own network.

He talks to the production houses, he talks to the actor and they confirm that OK you work on this project, we will join you and therefore it is easy for him.

Most of the films which are released recently are writer, director movies and the product also comes good because the director has a vision when he is writing the script.

He knows what he wants out of it.

He knows the budget, he knows what star cast he wants and therefore it becomes easy. Most of these films also do well on the box office are writer, director movies.

You have to have at least one of them before you venture into film production and therefore the product that has to be sold becomes very important.

I told you the three ways there, there can be more than that today.

Now you have various options.

You can make a film for the Bollywood Film industry, Hindi language film.

You can make film for the OTT platform or you can make film even for the South Indian bilingual films.

Because now the South Indian films are being released simultaneously in regional language as well as dubbed Hindi versions and are doing great on the box office.

Therefore, most of the South Indian film makers are not selling their language rights in Hindi.

They are themselves directly releasing their film on the day one as it is released in all over India and therefore, we are getting all the pan India actors heroes from the South.

Whether it is Prabhas, NTR Junior, Yash, Ram Charan, Allu Arjun, Vijay Thalapathy all of them.

The top stars Pan Indian actors are coming from the South and in the future looks that this Pan India South Indian stars are going to take over the Hindi film industry.

All this information is important for commercial cinema, cinema for profit.

So, you have to plan even before writing the first word of the script.

You have to work on the project and you have to be very sure what the sources of revenues are and what is the kind of budget you are expecting for the film and what kind of returns you are expecting and the sources of the returns.

The best example of the fact that commercial film production is an altogether different ball game is the failure of Amitabh Bachchan production house ABCL. It is said that ABCL gave

many flops and incomplete films. Ever Rs 500 cheques issued were dishonoured. Amitabh Bachchan faced bankruptcy!!!

CHAPTER 27

In the news.
Keeping Nirnayak Hot.

There is no doubt about the fact that the film has to be kept hot and in the news all through till its release and in particular the publicity part has to be aggressive in the three to four months prior to release through print publicity, newspaper publicity, electronic media and now social media channels.

Newspapers and Film Magazines publicity is a very important component.

I remember myself having written more than fifty articles for the various newspapers Punjab Kesari, Amar Ujala, Dainik Tribune, The Hindustan Times, and the trade and film magazines including Filmfare.

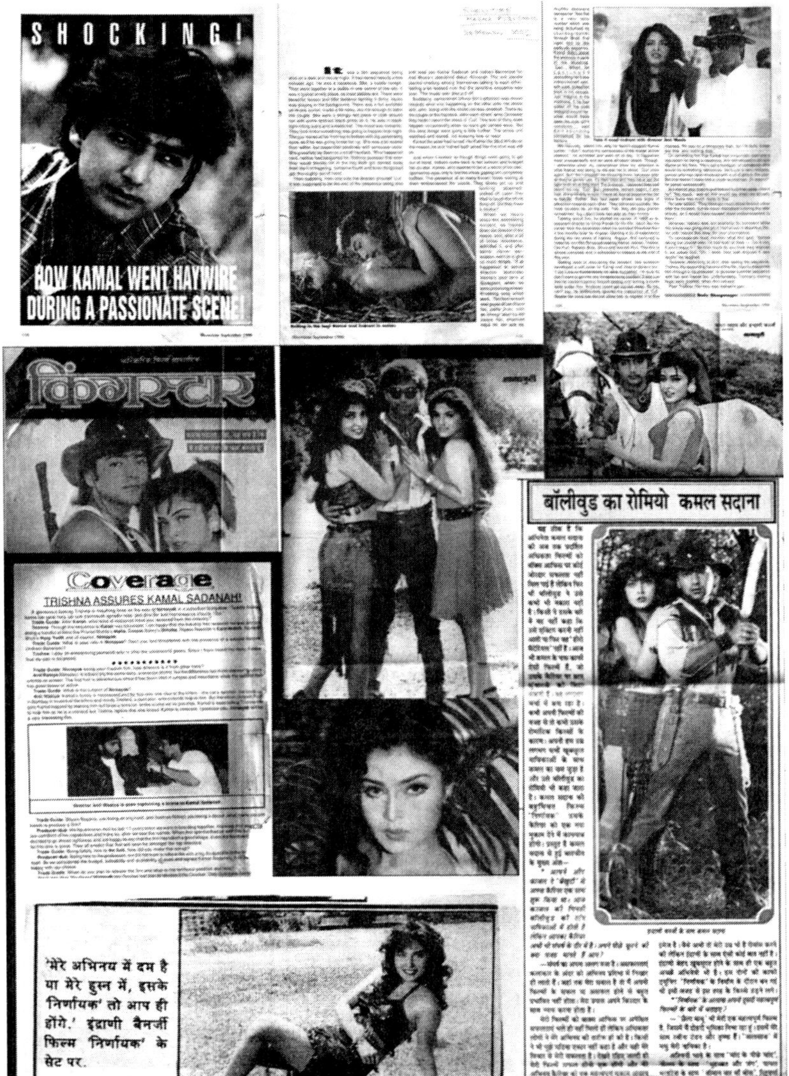
SHOCKING!
HOW KAMAL WENT HAYWIRE DURING A PASSIONATE SCENE!
Coverage
TRISHNA ASSURES KAMAL SADANAH!
बॉलीवुड का रोमियो कमल सदाना
'मेरे अभिनय में दम है या मेरे हुस्न में, इसके 'निर्णायक' तो आप ही होंगे.' इंद्राणी बैनर्जी फिल्म 'निर्णायक' के सेट पर.

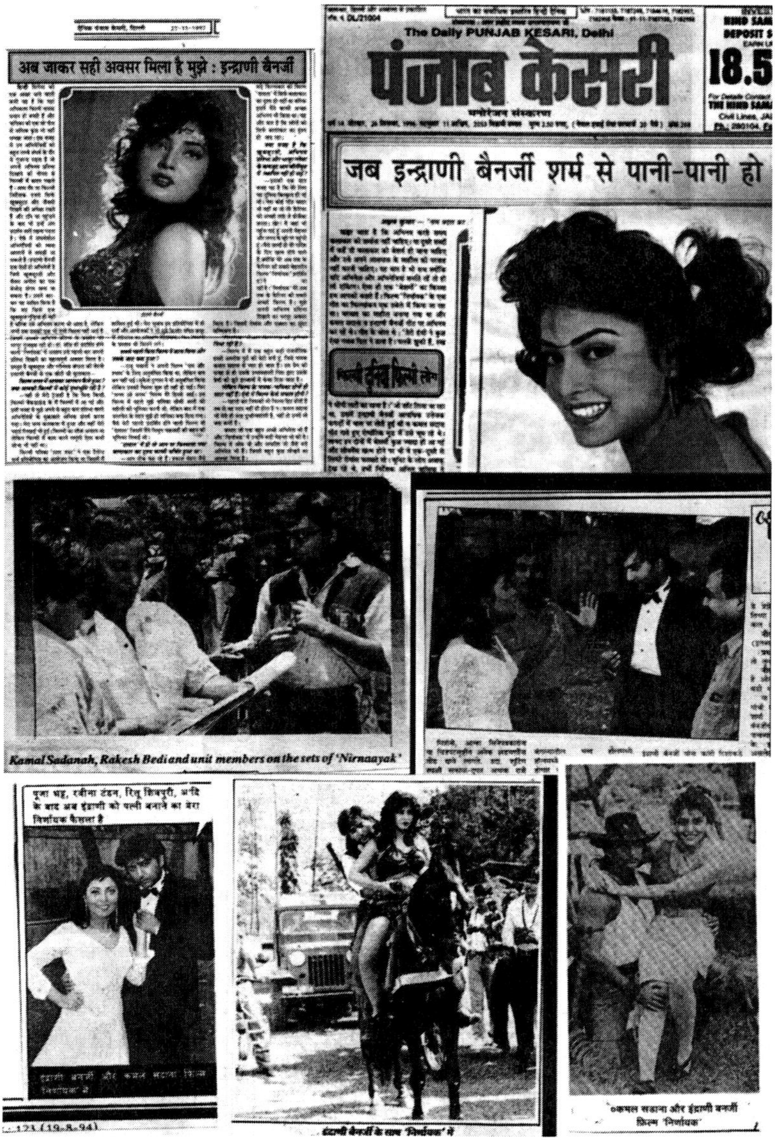

अब जाकर सही अवसर मिला है मुझे : इन्द्राणी बैनर्जी

The Daily PUNJAB KESARI, Delhi

पंजाब केसरी

जब इन्द्राणी बैनर्जी शर्म से पानी-पानी हो

Kamal Sadanah, Rakesh Bedi and unit members on the sets of 'Nirnaayak'

पूजा भट्ट, रवीना टंडन, रितू शिवपुरी, आदि के बाद अब इंद्राणी को पत्नी बनाने का मेरा निर्णायक फैसला है

इंद्राणी बनर्जी और कमल सदाना फिल्म 'निर्णायक' में

123 (19-8-94)

इंद्राणी बैनर्जी के साथ 'निर्णायक' में

कमल सदाना और इंद्राणी बनर्जी फिल्म 'निर्णायक'

And you have to keep it active in the entertainment channels, social media platforms, in terms of releasing the trailer of the film, releasing the songs of the film and keeping the movie hot in the news so that it helps the initial week at least to pull the masses to theatres to watch the film.

In our case, the very fact that it was the first ever film of Clash of Titans, Om Puri and Amrish Puri was highlighted.

More than hundred articles on their Clash were published in various newspapers and magazines.

Then we also created some articles.

All articles about a film or the relationship between the hero and the heroine or similar kind of gossips are needed and are important to keep the film in the news which helps in the box office collection and also in the long run when the film is released on the satellite TV channels and VCR.

All these modalities, whether it is news or some important article in the magazines, in the newspapers, on the TV channels, on the satellite channels and now of course on the OTT platforms is very important to give a good price and a good box office collection of the film.

Remember "Out of sight, out of mind."

CHAPTER 28

Preparing for release – Nirnayak our baby

Nirnayak is our baby says Bollywood family

Having finally received the censor certificate from the Censor Board, which was an A certificate we were with Manmohan Shetty, Adlabs Films, our processing lab.

Manmohan Shetty, Director Adlabs was to prepare the first print of the movie Nirnayak and release of number of prints as demanded by the distributors.

I and Anil Wasia were sitting in front of Manmohan Shetty and he calculated that about 30 lakhs for the dues which have to be cleared before the 1st print of the film could be released.

These 30 lakhs included the raw stock and processing charges.

ADLABS

FILMS PVT. LTD.

35/38, SUREN ROAD, ANDHERI (EAST), BOMBAY-400 093. TEL.: 8367705 ☐ FAX: 836 77 27

Mr. Kamal Sadanah,
Jal Kamal, Plot No. 22, T.P.S.III,
28th Road, Bandra (West),
MUMBAI 400 050

Ref : A-61/LG/717/9
23rd July, 1996.

COPY

Dear Sir,

Re : Film **'NIRNAYAK'** by M/s. Aryama Pictures Pvt. Ltd.
Directed by : Anil Hamirwasiya   Starring : Om Puri, Amrish Puri & Others

As per the irrevocable instructions of M/s. Aryama Pictures Pvt. Ltd., Mumbai, vide their letter dated 19.7.96 we hereby agree to collect a sum of **Rs. 2,24,000/- (RUPEES TWO LAKHS TWENTY FOUR THOUSAND ONLY)** from the producer or distributors before delivering the release prints of the above film for theatrical release in **MUMBAI, DELHI-UP. AND BENGAL CIRCUIT whichever is earlier** as known in the film trade and on receipt of the same we shall pay to you.

We further confirm not to deliver any release prints of the above film for theatrical release in **MUMBAI, DELHI-U.P. AND BENGAL CIRCUIT whichever is earlier** as known in the film trade to any party including M/s. Aryama Pictures Pvt. Ltd., till such time we receive the amount of **Rs. 2,24,000/- (RUPEES TWO LAKHS TWENTY FOUR THOUSAND ONLY)** from them on your behalf.

However nothing in this arrangement shall in any manner affect our first paramount lien and charge on the said picture and sound negatives as also all other rights for recovery of the general balance due in respect of the said film as well as the producers above named.

We shall not be responsible or liable in any manner if any print or prints delivered for any other purpose are directly or indirectly released in the above said circuit or part thereof without our consent.

In the event the producers have created or hereinafter create any rights in favour of third party/parties without our consent which may adversely affect your rights or interest then we shall not in any manner be held responsible or liable for the same.

We shall not be bound or in any manner liable or responsible hereunder in the event of our being required and/or ordered to deliver the negatives and/or ordered to deliver the release prints of the above said film to any person whatsoever in pursuance of any order or direction of court of law or any government authority including income Tax Authorities.

O[illegible]ligations to you under this letter of confirmation are limited to the extent and manner mentioned [illegible]bove. Please confirm your acceptance of above terms and conditions in corporating your specimen sig[illegible]ure which is a must for all future reference and guidance to us failing which this confirmation letter shall not be binding on us, which please note.

Thanking you,
Yours truly,
for ADLABS FILMS PVT. LTD.

DIRECTOR
c.c.to : M/s. Aryama Pictures Pvt. Ltd., Mumbai.

I agree and confirm the above

MR. KAMAL SADANAH

Kamal Sadanah

M/s. Adlabs Films Pvt. Ltd.,
35/38, Suren Road,
Andheri (East),
Mumbai - 400 093.

ADLABS
...ed. the Original
On...6/10/97...

Dear Sirs,

Sub.: Lab Guarantee/Letter against film 'NIRNAYAK'
Produced by M/s. Aryama Pictures Pvt. Ltd.,

In reference to the above mentioned subject, you have issued me a Lab Guarantee vide your letter dated 23rd July 1996 your Ref. No. A-61/LG/717/9 for an amount of Rs. 2,24,000/- which is due to me from M/s. Aryama Pictures Pvt. Ltd.

Considering the status of the film 'NIRNAYAK' I am forgoing the said amount of Rs. 2,24,000/-.

Kindly be hereby directed to cancel the above referred Lab Guarantee issued to me and please send the confirmation of the same to M/s. Aryama Pictures Pvt. Ltd.

Thanking you,

Yours Truely,

5/10/97

Jai Kamal, Plot No. 202, T.P.S. III, 28th Road, Bandra (West), Bombay-400 050. ☎ 6427389

(1)

COPY

Mr. Amrish Puri,
Vardaan, Plot No.45, J.V.P.D.Scheme,
MUMBAI 400 049.

Ref : A-61/LG/362/96
18th April, 1996.

Dear Sir,

Re : Film "NIRNAYAK" produced by M/s. Aryama Pictures Pvt. Ltd.
Directed by : Anil Hamirwasiya
Starring : Kamal Sadhana & Others

As per the irrevocable instructions of M/s. Aryama Pictures P. Ltd., Mumbai, vide their letter dated 17.4.96 we hereby agree to collect a sum of Rs. 4,00,000/- (Rupees Four Lakhs Only) from the producer or distributors before delivering the release prints of the above film for theatrical release in **ANY INDIAN CIRCUIT** as known in the film trade and on receipt of the same we shall pay to you.

We further confirm not to deliver any release prints of the above film for theatrical release in **ANY INDIAN CIRCUIT** as known in the film trade to any party including M/s. Aryama Pictures Pvt. Ltd., till such time we receive the amount of Rs. 4,00,000/- (Rupees Four Lakhs Only from them on your behalf.

However nothing in this arrangement shall in any manner affect our first paramount lien and charge on the said picture and sound negatives as also all our other rights for recovery of the general balance due in respect of the said film as well as the producers above named.

We shall not be responsible or liable in any manner if any print or prints delivered for any other purpose are directly or indirectly release in the above said circuit or part thereof without our consent.

In the event, the producers have created or hereinafter create any rights in favour of Third party/parties without our consent which may adversely affect your rights or interest, then we shall not in any manner be held responsible or liable for the same.

We shall not be bound or in any manner liable or responsible hereunder in the event of our being required and/or ordered to deliver the negatives and/or ordered to deliver the release prints of the above said film to any person whatsoever in pursuance of any order or direction of court of law or any government authority including income tax authorities.

Our obligations to you under this letter of confirmation are limited to the extent and manner mentioned hereinabove.

Please confirm your acceptance of above terms and conditions in corporating your specimen signature, which is a must for all future reference and guidance to us failing which this confirmation letter shall not be binding on us, which please note.

Thanking you,

Yours truly,
for **ADLABS FILMS PVT. LTD.**

DIRECTOR

I agree and confirm the above

MR. AMRISH PURI

c.c.to : M/s. Aryama Pictures P. Ltd., Mumbai.

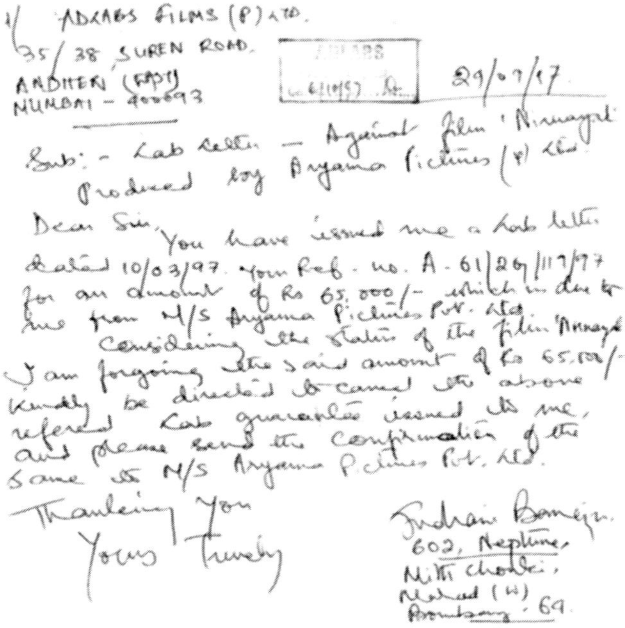

To
ADLABS FILMS (P) LTD.
35/38, SUREN ROAD,
ANDHERI (EAST)
MUMBAI - 400093

29/07/97

Sub:- Lab letter — Against film 'Nirnayak' Produced by Aryama Pictures (P) Ltd.

Dear Sir,
You have issued me a lab letter dated 10/03/97. Your Ref. no. A-61/269/11/7/97 for an amount of Rs 65,000/- which is due to me from M/S Aryama Pictures Pvt. Ltd.
Considering the status of the film 'Nirnayak' I am forgoing the said amount of Rs 65,000/-
Kindly be directed to cancel the above referred Lab guarantee issued to me, and please send the confirmation of the same to M/S Aryama Pictures Pvt. Ltd.

Thanking you
Yours Truly

Indrani Banerjee
602, Neptune,
Mithi Chowki,
Malad (W)
Bombay - 64.

The negative charges of adlabs and also included the lab letters issued to various actors and technicians amounts to be paid before the first print could be released.

Manmohan Shetty told us that he has got more than 400 films in the garbage box.

Films which were incomplete, 4 reels, 5 reels, 6 reels and also films which were complete but did not get the censor certificate. For example, there was a film which was on animals with Juhi Chawla as an actress and because of the torture to animals it never received the censor certificate and it never got released and remained in the boxes.

There were other films which got the censor certificate.

But because of certain legal and financial issues including dispute between the producers, the producer and directors pending in various courts and other legal issues in the various courts, even the censored films could not be released.

And these included the films of superstars even like the Khans and the Kapoors, even Sunny Deol.

Jokingly, he told me that since 400 films are in the garbage box never to be released, Nirnayak can also end up there if the dues are not paid.

He then asked me how many prints do you intend to release the film with and after adding the total with the various distributors who had booked for the different circuits and territories, it came out to be 64 prints. One print cost at that time was about Rs 50,000.
And he said that our dues will be recovered from the prints as the payment of the prints is done by the distributors.

And later on, because the films territories, most of them were on minimum guarantee basis, they recover the money of the prints, their own expenses, publicity and then whenever there is the complete recovery, the extra income is called overflow and the overflow is to be shared equally between the producers and the distributors.

If you promise me 64 prints, whatever dues against me, they can be covered up. I will handle them.

But then what about the dues of actors and technicians against the lab letters.

I discussed with Anil regarding what to do and we decided to approach each and every actor and technician, whose amounts, the portion of their professional fees, the numeration was due against the lab letter and request them to cancel their lab letters and withdraw their lab letters in the interest of the film to be released.

So, one by one I visited Kamal Sadanah, Indrani Banerjee, Om Puri, Amrish Puri, our cameraman Ishwar Bidri and others.

There were many other amounts, small amounts, which were due against lab letters.

Lab letter is a surety to the actors and the technician, that a portion of their fees of their acting or technical remunerations which are to be paid before the film is released which is around could be 25-30% of the total fees.

And as we approached them, I was personally very sceptical whether all these people will agree to withdraw their lab letter in the interest of the film release.

But to my pleasant shock each and every one cooperated and issued the letter to the lab that they are cancelling their lab letter and withdrawing the demand for money which is due to them against the lab letter in the larger interest so that the film

gets released which includes Om Puri, Kamal Sadanah, Indrani Banerjee, Ishwar Bidri, the cameraman. Almost every major actor and technician had a lab letter and so we were able to get the cancellation of the lab letter and the film was ready to be released.

Amrish Puri did not cancel the Lab Letter issued to him because at the time of release he was charging 20X the fees we signed him for. But I thank him as he did not insist on raising his fees. Many Bollywood Insiders would have blackmailed the producers in such a situation.

No big actor, the Khan, the Kapoor, Ajay Devgan or Akshay Kumar could make a film without the main villain opposite them being Amrish Puri.

And as you know, Om Puri had to be a part of many big budget films and you would be surprised that the cost of our filmmaking when it was ready to be released was almost equal to the renumeration which Amrish Puri was getting per film at that time!!!

And both of them knew that the film was getting released only because of them and the fees they had signed for was meagre in front of their fees they were charging today.

And I repeat, they never ever said that since your film is being released because of me, you increase the renumeration and I will not withdraw the lab letters.

They never blackmailed us and the entire acting and technical crew were very cooperative.

This was a surprise for me. Here was the clearcut evidence that Bollywood apart from 1% of nepotism, Vanshwadi and insiders is largely a family of great people.

The Bollywood is a single large family and everybody cooperates in the interest of the project.

The film which is their baby, a film is the baby of not only the producer, the director, the actors, the technician, but everybody involved including the spot boy.

So that's the beauty of Bollywood.

And so ultimately with the lab letter being withdrawn with 64 prints confirmed to be released, the first print of the of our film Nirnayak was ready to be released.

CHAPTER 29

Preparing for release – The breakdown

Overwork catches up.

After setting everything in place, the film was ready to be released on 26th December 1997 and 2nd of January 1998, Sometime in the first week of December, I came back to Delhi to have a short rest.

I happened to attend a wedding party where suddenly I fell down and became unconscious.

I was taken to the National Heart Institute where they checked that my blood pressure was slightly high.

All other parameters were normal.

And then they took the history and the ultimate diagnosis was that because of this overwork, because of the hard work day

and night, the stress, the tension associated with the making and the release of the film, I was suffering from severe exhaustion and they advised me total bed rest.

I came home and in the next week the same thing happened twice with me.

I was standing and suddenly I fell down feeling dizzy and then lay down in the bed. The date of the film release 26th December was approaching and I was on bed in Delhi.

My Co producers Ashok Verma from Delhi and Shyam Bagaria from Calcutta and our director Anil Wasia, came to Delhi to visit me and they told my parents that Sushrut has to come to Bombay because without him it will not be possible to release the film. As many things are to be done.

The Prints have to be planned. They have to be dispatched to 14 different locations and lot of paperwork is also needed to be done.

The print publicity also has to be dispatched.

So, he has to come to Bombay but seeing my health condition, my parents and my wife, they refused.

They said he is not in a healthy condition.

You all go and release the movie. His health condition does not permit Sushrut to travel to Bombay.

Anil told my family that it is impossible to release the film until and unless Sushrut comes to Bombay and takes over the entire process of releasing the film.

And they promised that they will take full care of me.

After a few deliberations, it was decided that I would be taken by wheelchair to the Bombay Rajdhani train.

And from Bombay Central I got down on wheelchair and reached our Office cum house, at Lokhandwala. Pagers had arrived by then and the entire process of a successful worldwide theatrical release of Nirnayak – The Decider, I organised and managed while lying in bed.

CHAPTER 30

A film is really made on the editing table

After making Nirnayak, I realized that the most important technical part of film making is editing.

Editing. They say that the film is made on the editing table.

Editing can upgrade average shot film and downgrade A beautifully shot film.

Wrong editing can destroy a good film.

Good editing can make an average film look too good, because the purpose of editing is that not a single frame which is not needed is kept in the film.

Forget about the scenes.

Even if a single frame is looking extra, it is to be removed and it has to be so cut that the film goer doesn't get even a second to think beyond the film.

And that is the mastery of editing.

I think one of the actors whose films are very well edited is Aamir Khan.

There is not a single frame, not a single shot, not a single scene which looks that it could be removed from the film, it is so engrossing that when the film starts and when the film ends, one does not realise because of very good editing.

There is no lengthy stretching of any scene and it is cut to cut.

So editing is a very important aspect and I believe that if you watch Nirnayak, our **editor Naresh Ambastha** did a really good job.

And during editing I was sitting with him and the director Anil was sitting and we took special care that not a single scene, not a single frame which was not needed in the film is there.

Just watch Nirnayak and you will appreciate what I have explained.

Lots of editors contribute to the success or failure of a film.

CHAPTER 31

Mixing, Creating the Mood of the scene

I think mixing is another important part of filmmaking.

A very undervalued part of filmmaking.

Because it is this which really sets the mood of the scene.

Whether the scene is one of suspense, comedy, adventure or of action, whatever the scene, it is the sound mixing which is important and creates a great impact.

And what happens in sound mixing is that in the mixing studio there are many soundtracks.

I think minimum 4 soundtracks, but I have seen even 10-12 soundtracks.

One soundtrack is the dialogue, another soundtrack could be the background music and background score, and the third soundtrack could be the sounds of a moving vehicle or a siren of ambulance or maybe chirping of the birds.

And you can have any number of soundtracks running parallel, and the sound creates a very important impact on the audience.

I have experienced that these are the three aspects of the film.

When we are watching a film, there is a video, the visual part movie.

Then there are dialogues which the different actors are saying.

And then there is this background music or background score.

And then all these sounds like the siren of an ambulance or a police vehicle or a road accident or sound of bursting clouds, raining, chirping of the birds.

And these are multiple tracks which are running together simultaneously.

I realized that, if I switched off the video, concentrate on the sound the dialogues, then remove the dialogues, and just on the background music and the siren and other things.

And I realized that among all these three things, the background score and the sound effects which are produced like the chirping of the birds or the road accident or impending danger or comedy sound, they are the most

important, more important than even the dialogues and the scenes which are running.

Mixing becomes very important.

It was while we were mixing the soundtracks and watching the movie on the screen, I realized how important it is the role of mixing when a particular aspect of the sound, whether dialogue, whether background or whether these sound effects are increased or decreased depending upon the effect these sounds have to have to impact the mood of the entire scene and impacts therefore the audience and keeps them hooked to the movie.

CHAPTER 32

Some interesting facts

When we were deciding, planning the selection, casting the actors for various roles, the role of Inspector Nanak came to our mind. As you would realise the character of Inspector Nanak is very crucial to the film. (Later during nomination for the best supporting role in various cine awards we sent the name of Om Puri who finally played the role of Inspector Nanak)

Who should play the role of Inspector Nanak?

Anil Wasia, who had worked with Nana Patekar in Angaar, suggested his name and went to Nana Patekar. He said that he was not interested and he forwarded us to Nasiruddin Shah.

When we went to Nasiruddin Shah, he said I have done a lot of inspector roles and he called Om Puri and said that there is a role of an inspector.

Then we want to Om Puri and ultimately Om Puri agreed to do the role of Inspector Nanak and later on when it came to the commercial part of filmmaking, we got the returns for casting him as Inspector Nanak.

Later on as I have mentioned earlier, I realized that we could have made it a two hero film with Kamal Sadanah as one hero and Saif Ali Khan who was a rising star at the time in 1993 as the other hero.

And this Inspector Nanak role would then be done by Saif Ali Khan.

As mentioned earlier, if during the making of the film, even if one of the actors films flop and he do not do well and other hero his film rises, then it will be good for the commercial aspect of the film.

Other thing I would like to share is that about piracy.

Piracy was very rampant and therefore we withheld the release of the VCR and the cable rights of the film.

We were willing to take a risk of about 2 1/2 lakhs on the VCR rights and the cable rights.

We didn't part with both the rights so that it does not affect the box office of the film and audio piracy.

Talking of the audio piracy one of my friends who was in the business of printing, showed me inlay card of an audio cassette and a sticker of VCR of Nirnayak The Decider which were in Urdu and were to be sent to Pakistan.

Because around the release of the film in theatres, the film was already popular in Pakistan and the piracy of the audio cassettes and the VCR was going on in Pakistan even in those times.

Other thing I would like to share is that it was a rare combination of film makers.

Three friends from Birla Public School Pilani with I being a medical doctor by profession, Shyam Bagaria, engineer from BITS Pilani and Anil Wasia was the director of the film did his law from Delhi Law College with no godfather in Bollywood, with zero knowledge of filmmaking and nil experience of filmmaking we ventured into making a Bollywood film Nirnayak and **every moment, every day was a first-time learning experience and we took in the learnings earnestly.**

We made note of everything that was happening.

Whether it was picturization of the song, recording of the song, erection of the set, shooting at various locations, every moment was a learning experience.

We picked up very quickly the nuances of filmmaking and most importantly the commercial aspect of how to make a successful commercial film and being able to sell it for theatrical release and worldwide theatrical release and various other satellite channels and other revenue generating options.

CHAPTER 33

The D Day at Maratha Mandir – As Kanpur shivers

Wait is over.

Maratha Mandir in Bombay near to the Bombay Central Railway Station is considered to be a very auspicious theatre for mahurat release of any film and it is very difficult to get this theatre.

But as we were forced to release the film during the month of Ramadan (incidentally there were two Ramadan months in the year 1997. This phenomenon happens every 33 years. Next it will happen in the year 2030) which started on the 30th of December 1997, Nirnayak was released in Bombay theatres on 2nd of January Friday, 1998.

Because in of the month of Ramadan, no Khan or Kapoor, or Akshay Kumar or Ajay Devgan release their film during the period of Ramadan because 30 to 40% of the theatre audience is the Muslim community and during the period of Ramadan, they don't normally watch a film in the theatre.

Because of that we did get Maratha Mandir to do our Mahurat screening.

The first show of the film which was the 12 noon show and myself and director Anil Wasia reached the Maratha Mandir at 11:30 am.

The house was almost 60 to 70% capacity occupied and we were looking through the small hole in the projector room that the audience was arriving and just prior to starting the film we did the Ganesh Pooja and broke the coconut and the film was released.

We stayed there during the first screening of the film at Maratha Mandir and it was really very encouraging when people were whistling or clapping, particularly at the Om Puri versus Amrish Puri scenes.

Another thing I would like to share is the difficulty in the month of January of making the prints reach the theatres because of severe cold wave, fog and disruption of air and rail services.

We got a call from the distributor from Kanpur on the first night that because of the fog the planes are not taking off or landing and the print has to reached by 11 am because the theatres are booked and if the film is not started at 12 noon at the Kanpur theatres, people who have booked the tickets would throw stones and damage the cinema hall.

Because first day first show is a very sensitive and important show.

The people who are real lovers of films, they watch every movie FDFS. The first day first show ones are the real fanatics.
We didn't know what to do and then we thought of a solution.

The plane landed at Delhi Airport with the Prints and from Delhi to Kanpur all through the night in the foggy weather by road, the Prints were taken to Kanpur and other cities of UP and luckily, they reached there on time before the scheduled release of the film at 12 noon and people were able to watch the movie on time.

These are things which are very crucial when you release a film and sometimes instant decisions have to be taken.

And as said earlier also it is very tricky because the theatres are booked and particularly for a first day show, people are very crazy, very eagerly waiting for the film.

And if the film is not released then they get very angry and even violent sometimes.

So luckily the film reached Kanpur and was released and the audience really applauded and enjoyed the film.

Despite being released worldwide in theatres in 1997/98, almost 27 years after its release Nirnayak looks contemporary to the present times as evidenced by its popularity on youtube with more than 16 lakh views and rave comments and an excellent IMDB score of 7/10.

CHAPTER 34

About Nepotism in Bollywood Vanshwaad, Insiders and Outsiders

Did Nirnayak suffer from nepotism?

And the answer is yes in many ways.

Let me first define nepotism for you.
Nepotism is not that a vanshwadi and insider star kid does not become an actor.

Nepotism happens when a vanshwadi and insider steals great scripts written for outsiders by blackmailing the producers, directors and writers.

Nepotism happens when films of outsiders are deliberately shelved after a few scenes to destroy their careers.

ARYAMA
PICTURES PVT. LTD.
9, Shanti Bhuvan, Chapel Lane,
Santacruz (W), Bombay - 400054
Tel: [illegible]

To Divya Datta,
Bandra (West),
Bombay.

Dated: [illegible]

With reference to the personal talks the Undersigned had with you, this day and the settlement arrived at between ourselves, this is to put on record that we have engaged to work and you have agreed to work as a Lead Actress in our forthcomming film in Hindi tentatively titled as [illegible] being produced by [illegible] and directed by Anil Hamirvasiya and on the terms and conditions stipulated herein :-

1 That the Actress agrees to work as an Artiste in the said FIRST FILM directed by Anil Hamirvasia and further any two films after the said First Film as and when desired by the Company or its nominees. In consideration of the services to be rendered by the Actress persuant to this agreement for the said three films the Company agrees to pay the Actress as under:
a Rs 1,11,000/- (Rupees One Lakh Eleven Thousand only) for the first film, Rs.2,00,000/- (Rupees Two Lakh only) for the second film and Rs. 3,00,000/- (Rupees Three Lakh only) for the third film, being the total remunerations for the first, second and third films respectively, to be paid in easy installments to be decided ~~by the company~~.

[illegible] from today and shall and when the picture is finally completed, censored and released all over India. How,ever, in case we require your services even after the release of the picture for re-shooting or for any other purpose, you agree and undertake to complete such work without demanding any extra payment other than what is provided for herein.

3 That you have agreed to perform your duties to the best of your ability and to our entire satisfaction as demanded by the script and or the director. That you have agreed to give us the first preference as well as every co-operation for an early completion of the picture

cont..../.

Regd. Off.: C-39, East Of Kailash, New Delhi - 110065, Ph. 634455
Calcutta Off.: 6/3C, Lower Circular Road, Calcutta - 700017, Ph. 473240

-/ 2 /-

ARYAMA
PICTURES PVT. LTD.
9, Shanti Bhuvan, Chapel Lane,
Santacruz (W), Bombay-400054.
Tel.: 6491802

and that you will attend to your duties regularly as and when and where required and directed by us.

4 That in case we require services outside Bombay, you agree and undertake to accompany the unit to any Outdoor Location fixed by us. However, suitable travelling, lodging and boarding arrangements shall be made at our expenses.

5 That the Copy-Rights in respect of your entire work in the said picture and the words/lyrics/dialogues spoken etc. by you therein will be our absolute property and we shall be entitled to exploit the same for our own advantage and in whatever manner we think fit.

6 That the Income-Tax and/or any other taxes, if any, on the aforesaid remuneration shall be borne and paid by you directly to the concerned authorities and we shall not be responsible for the same.

7 That in case of any dispute of whatever kind between us arising out of and relating to this Agreement at any time the same shall be refferred to All India Film Producers Council, Bombay and/or to the Court/Courts of Greater Bombay, which shall have only jurisdiction to hear all or any disputes between us.

8 That the Company is entitled to dub and / or cause to be dubbed your voice in any language of its choice with the voice of any other artistes, if necessary in the said film.

9 That all other terms and conditions are as usual as prevailing in the Film Trade.

Kindly confirm the above.

Yours faithfully,
For Aryama Pictures Private Limited

(Anil Ramirwala)
Director

I confirm the above.

Divya Dutta 7/9/93

Regd. Off.: C-39, East Of Kailash, New Delhi - 110065, Ph.: 634455
Calcutta Off.: 6/3C, Lower Circular Road, Calcutta - 700017. Ph.: 473240

Nepotism is creating situations for the outsiders where they are forced to go into depression to the extent of committing suicides "abetment to suicide".

Nepotism happens when outsiders are forced to sign agreements and contracts which have clauses that damage their careers. Outsiders become puppets in the hands of the producers. Contracts may include clauses like "You will not sign any other film before our film is released OR Until our film is released no other film of yours will be released" and trap the innocent outsiders.

Incidentally we also had a clause in our contract with actress Divya Dutta that you will work with us in three movies on fixed renumeration whatever your market value. I feel all this is not in good taste. Though Divya Dutta was not later selected in the cast of Nirnayak.

Nepotism happens when dates of busy actors blocked with outsiders are given to established directors and producers.

Nepotism happens when outsiders are blocked from releasing films during festivals, long weekends holidays and in high footfall theatres.

Nepotism happens when vanshwadi and insiders don't allow outsiders to become super stars demanding 30-50 crore per film as they climb the ladder into top 10 heroes. They are ok as long as the outsider falls into a bracket of 2-4 crore per film and apply hook or crook means to prevent the rise of outsiders to the top.
Nepotism is evident when in the last 30 years only the likes of vanshvadi and insiders Khans, Kapoors, Bachchans, Bhatts, Akshay Kumar, Ajay Devgan occupy the Top 10 actors list. Not a single hero from J&K, Haryana, Uttar Pradesh, Madhya

Pradesh, Bengal or even South India in top 10 heroes of Bollywood.

However, since 2020 South Indian Pan India stars like Yash, Allu Arjun, Prabhas, Ram Charan, NTR Jr, Vijay are taking over hindi cinema.

Talking of nepotism, everyone is aware of the likes of Khans, Kapoors, Bhatts, Akhtars as vanshwadi and insiders.

Amitabh Bachchan could be one of the early promoters of Bollywood nepotism. It is often discussed in Bollywood circles that he being close to the most powerful family, the Gandhi family of India, Indira Gandhi and later Rajiv Gandhi promoting him in Bollywood in the 70s and 80s. Even after giving a series of flops in early part of his career, he continued to get roles.

But the real Vanshwaad, Parivarwaad, BhaiBhatijaVaad took off in the early 90s when Salman Khan, Shahrukh Khan, Saif Ali Khan, Aamir Khan, the Kapoors, Akshay Kumar, Ajay Devgan, Bobby Deol, all the star kids entered Bollywood.

This was in early 1990s. By the time NIRNAYAK, was ready for being released in the end of 1997 they had already become stars and super stars.

This Nepotism of vanshwad and insiders had taken over the entire Bollywood.

All the Festival Fridays, New Year, Christmas, Eid, Diwali release dates, were taken over and blocked for the release of these star kids, the Nepotism kids.

So for a non-Khan movie, a non-Kapoor movie or non-Akshay Kumar movie, a non-Ajay Devgan movie, it was impossible to get good dates of release, good theatres, theatres which are in prime location, great footfalls, near the railway stations, near the bus stands, in the markets, the malls which whatever the film is showing they will always have a good capacity.

So, when we were ready to release Nirnayak, we had to face this problem, our distributors told us that no theatres, no good theatres are available and the only option which was left to us was to release the film in the month of Ramadan.

Since 20 to 30% of the theatre going cinema lovers are from the Muslim community, none of these Bollywood Insiders and star kids dare to release their film during the month of Ramadan and so that is the only time when you can hope of releasing your films in good theatres across India. With 64 prints in different territories across India, we needed 64 good theatres to release Nirnayak for best results at box office.

So, then we only had the Ramadan period to release the film and therefore Nirnayak was released on the 2nd of January 1998 which was a Friday and which was the 4th day of the Ramadan month starting on the 30th of December 1997. In some territories NIRNAYAK was released on 26th December 1997.

We lost a huge Muslim cinema lovers in the process and it affected our box office collections to a great extent.

Another important issue we faced from nepotism was that when we had signed Om Puri and Amrish Puri in 1993 were not that popular but by 1997 both of them were hot properties, hot actors.

Amrish Puri after Dilwale Dulhania Le Jayenge in 1995 was pitted as a villain against every star kid, every superstar.

And it was very difficult to get dates of Amrish Puri and Om Puri and almost impossible to get their combined dates.

With almost six to seven scenes of Om Puri versus Amrish Puri pitted against each other, it was a herculean task to get their combined dates.

Sometimes we had to wait for six to seven months, to get their combined dates and after getting those dates we would receive the threatening calls from certain big production houses that release Om Puri and Amrit Puri for their shooting.

But we were adamant and we told them we already have to wait for six months for their dates and we will not be able to spare them during those days.

The major reason for this nepotism was the shifting of the concept of a box office collection.

While earlier it was the number of weeks a film was showed in the theatre and we calling them a silver Jubilee, if it was 25 weeks continuously on a theatre or a Golden Jubilee for 50 weeks.

Now the concept of film releases shifted to the new concept of stars so-called as crowd pullers.

It shifted to the opening weekend collection from number of weeks that is the opening Friday, Saturday, Sunday and the concept was to get a star hero and recover the entire amount in the first week of release, based on his brand value to pull the crowd. Content became a secondary issue.

Whether the content of the film is good or bad does not matter because star or the actor or the hero was the main puller and the film was released in maximum number of theatres across India to get the maximum first week collections.

So that people just because of the star value or the star pull, the actor pulls not the content pull go to the theatres booked Friday, Saturday, Sunday and by the time the reviews comes that the film is a useless movie with a very poor content they have recovered their investments by fooling the audience.

The producer has earned his money, making fool of the public with poor content and recovered the money and that practice continued for many years. Later on, because of this concept, the star fees, the actor fees also rose and there were times when the top ten heroes earned from 50 to 80% of the total income of the film.

Actors like Aamir Khan, Shahrukh Khan, they would charge up to 70 crore, 80 crore in 100 crore film and if they are not getting the 80 crore, then they would launch their own production company and take the rights, the distribution rights of the film to the extent of 80% of the movie.

The real producer who was taking the risks and investing the money or the production house was putting the money was getting only up to 15% to 20% and 80% was taken home by the hero after adjusting the distributor and exhibitor theatre owner share.

And all this astronomical rise in star fees resulted in nepotism, vanshvad where the insiders did not allow the outsiders to become a 50-crore per film actor.

And these star kids and nepotism kids, the Bollywood insiders bullied the producers, directors, writers and outsider actors, so nepotism and Vanshwaad prospered.

By late 1990s because 80% of the income was booked by the superstar and therefore these Khans, Kapoors, Akshay Kumars and Ajay Devgan's never allowed any outsider to enter the top ten and would do anything by hook or crook to prevent outsiders rise to the top and enter the 50 crore per film bracket.

Maybe steal their scripts, maybe not allow their film to be completed, maybe not allow them good theatres so that nobody ever attempts or dares to enter the top ten.

Because the moment you enter top 10, your fees rose above 10 crore, 20 crore, 30 crores and therefore nepotism was a big issue when NIRNAYAK was released and we suffered at the box office because of this nepotism and our collections were affected. Still

NIRNAYAK did a good business at the box office and it was a successful film at the box office.

It is also important to define "Outsiders "in the present context.
Influential wealthy people, celebrity kids are also not Outsiders. From this standpoint Amitabh Bachchan, Shah Rukh Khan, Akshay Kumar are not outsiders. Even Deepika Padukone is not an outsider. Ranveer Singh and Kirti Sanon are not outsiders by any means.
A chaiwala, bus conductor, school teacher, a common Indian, aam aadmi or his kid qualifies for being a genuine outsider. Kartik Aaryan, Rajkummar Rao fall in this category of real genuine outsiders. Kangna Ranaut is a genuine outsider.

Technically, the South Indian Stars and Super Stars, also fall into the category of Real Genuine Bollywood Outsiders for Bollywood Insiders and Vanshwaadis and were given the same ill treatment from 1990 to 2020. It was the North India release of Hindi Dubbed version of Bahubali in 2020 which changed everything. As recent as 2023, as per social media posts, Shah Rukh Khan unsuccessfully tried his best to block the release of a Prabhas starrer Salaar Part 1 in north India theatres the release of which was clashing with the release of Shah Rukh Khan starrer Dunki.

CHAPTER 35

Was NIRNAYAK – The Decider a box office success?

Box Office

COLLECTION STATEMENT OF PICTURE "NIRNAYAK"

NAME OF HALL	CAPACITY	FRIDAY	SATURDAY	SUNDAY	MONDAY	TUESDAY	WEDNESDAY	THURSDAY	WEEKLY TOTAL
PARADISE, CALCUTTA	10,630.80	11,468.65	9,945.40	22,891.05	10,717.15	9,311.35	9,309.25	11,933.80	85,576.65
MAJESTIC, CALCUTTA	8,905.40	9,833.40	5,644.90	18,073.60	7,103.00	7,352.90	5,563.50	3,698.00	57,269.30
LIBERTY, CALCUTTA	4,371.50	7,598.50	5,619.00	12,242.00	4,665.50	3,771.00	3,463.00	4,154.00	41,513.00
KRISHNA, CALCUTTA	7,471.35	3,719.40	4,144.80	13,445.35	3,806.15	3,552.60	3,741.85	2,718.45	35,128.60
NATIONAL, KHIDERPORE	4,113.00	9,659.68	6,721.12	11,017.76	6,344.50	3,874.60	3,281.44	2,836.44	43,735.54
BHAWANI, TOLLYGUNGE	4,022.15	2,694.90	2,120.35	3,638.45	2,079.00	1,821.75	1,783.80	2,278.50	16,416.75
MRINALINI, DUM DUM		5,504.00	4,025.00	8,231.00	4,011.00	3,094.00	2,780.00	3,477.00	31,122.00
MAYAPURI, SHIBPUR	3,796.00	3,168.00	2,038.00	3,598.00	1,397.00	1,555.00	1,359.00	1,818.00	14,933.00
BANGOBASI, HOWRAH	7,481.85	8,095.95	5,550.75	11,062.20	7,860.00	4,777.95	4,041.00	5,575.20	46,963.05
RAKHI, SALKIA	6,494.15	2,953.80	3,096.30	8,467.10	3,830.80	4,392.90	3,035.25	6,155.70	31,931.85
ALLOCHAYA, BELIAGHATA	4,875.00	4,995.60	4,037.90	9,453.70	4,196.20	2,908.80	2,614.60	5,014.80	33,221.80

J. D. PICTURES

SUPER ART INTERNATIONAL

1495, 2nd Floor, Ram Gali, Film Colony, Bhagirath Palace, Chandni Chowk, Delhi-110006

Business Statement for the month of: APRIL '98

Submitted to Producers M/s. Aryama Pictures (P) Ltd, Mumbai

Name of Film: NIRNAYAK

Date: 15.5.98

Business upto month March '98: 5,12,766.95

Business of the Current month: 51,485.37

Total: 5,64,[illegible]

Kamal Raj International

203, MANJU MAHAL, 35, PALI HILL, BANDRA, BOMBAY-400 050. TEL.: 54 02 85

A/101, PANCHDHARA, OPP. YARI ROAD, VERSOVA, ANDHERI (W). MUMBAI 400 061.

Ref. No.

Date: 09/12/1997.

Raids on Piracy

TO WHOMSOEVER IT MAY CONCERN

We hereby confirm that we have authorised M/s. Universal Raid Campaign and their representatives having their office at Mansarovar Apts., Shop No. 4, B. P. Road, Bhayander (E). 401 105 to conduct raid on illegal screening, telecasting of our picture "KAUN ROKEGA MUJHE" in Hindi starring Chankey Pandey, Ragma, Gulshan Grover, Ranjeet, Prem Chopra, Suda Chandran, Shakti Kapoor, Govinda (Guest

ARORA SATNAM SINGH

ALL INDIA BOX OFFICE REPORTER

12th September 1994

Mr. Shyam Bagaria
and Dr Sushrut Almast,
M/S Aryama Pictures P.Ltd,
9, Shanti Bhuvan, Chapel Lane,
Santacruz (W),
BOMBAY 400 054

monitoring Box Office

Dear sir,

REF : YOUR FILM "NIRNAYAK"

At the out set I would like to congratulate you on nearing completion of your prestigious film "NIRNAYAK" in Hindi. My good wishes for its success at the Box Office.

After successful release, the performance and business of the film at various centres has to be carefully watched, monitored, analysed and assessed. This is necessary to ensure that a correct and truthful business of the film at various centres is being reported by the various distributors to the producer. This requires a great deal of experience and expertise. Person responsible for the overall monitoring and assessment of business at various centres should have a vast experience in distribution trade.

I am sure you would certainly require the services of an expert in the field to ensure correct reportage of business of your film at various centres and I am glad to offer my services for this work.

I have already undertaken the work for several successful releases like "PHOOL AUR KAANTE"., "SANAM"., "SADAK"., "SALAAMI"., "ANARI"., "PREM QAIDI"., "SAAJAN"., "AANKHEIN"., "BOL RADHA BOL"., "TRIDEV", "VISHWATMA"., "LAADLA"., "DILWALE" etc and my expertise in this field has yielded high benefits to the producers.

Apart from my vast experience and expertise, I am monitoring computer Data Bank of the terms and collections of several films at various centres for comparative analysis and this will greatly help in the assessment of business of your film at various centres.

A.B.C.L.'S FORAY INTO SOUTH

A.B.C.L. took its first step into the world of Southern music by releasing two Malayalam cassettes. The first cassette has the music of two films, INDRAPRASTAM and DILLIWALA RAJKUMAR. The second cassette, ONAM PONNONAM is an album of Onam festival songs. The cassettes were released in a celebrity-studded gathering on 10th August at Taj Coromandal in Madras. Amitabh Bachchan, Mammootty and Meena released the first cassette and the second was released by Mr. Bachchan, Mohanlal and Khushboo.

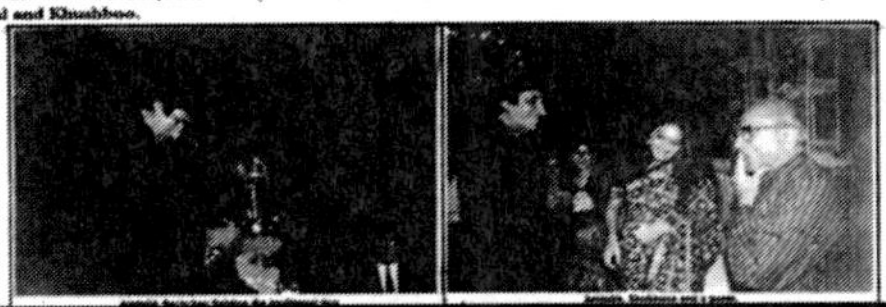

ABCL a production disaster by Amitabh Bachchan . Commercial Film Production is an altogether different ball game.

ALL-INDIA THEATRE CAPACITIES-1991

CINEMA	SEATS	CAPACITY PER SHOW	CAPACITY FOR 28 SHOWS	PHONE
		BOMBAY		
Ajanta (Borivli)	910	3,939.00	1,10,292.00	6010253
Akash (Kurla)	568	1,778.00	49,784.00	5141856
Alankar	1117	4,427.00	92,967.00	352655
Alankar (matinees)	—	2,661.00	18,627.00	354776
Amar (Chembur)	1223	2,980.75	83,461.00	5517016
Anand (Thana)	995	3,715.40	1,03,891.20	592985
Ankur (Gowandi)	1127	3,673.50	1,02,858.00	5519796
Aradhana (Thana)	1002	3,912.50	1,09,550.00	595077
Ashish (Chembur)	1000	4,296.78	1,20,310.00	5515255/9673
Ashok (Thana)	661	1,416.10	39,650.80	592155
Aurora	794	1,472.60	41,233.80	4071497
Alfred	938	1,670.00	46,760.00	358606/358262
Anupam (Goregaon)	927	3,089.10	86,494.80	6732044
Badal (Matunga)	1193	3,836.00	1,07,408.00	4307382
Bahar (Parle)	965	4,346.00	1,21,688.00	6342557/5887
Bandra Talkies	549	1,987.00	55,636.00	6423761
Basant (Chembur)	1009	4,213.00	1,17,964.00	5513852
Bharat (Kurla)	603	1,742.75	48,797.00	5125826
Bharatmata	756	1,440.10	40,322.80	4130673
Bijlee (Matunga)	880	2,793.00	78,204.00	4306613
Bhanu (Kalyan)	1020	3,234.50	90,566.00	9293366
Capitol (V.T.)	889	3,406.50	95,382.00	2041822
Central	862	1,859.00	39,039.00 (21 shows)	351277
Central (matinees)	—	1,579.60	11,057.20	351277
Chandan (Juhu)	1,295	4,357.50	1,22,010.00	6202296
Chitra (Dadar)	823	2,585.00	72,380.00	4112264
Citylight (Mahim)	747	1,607.35	45,005.80	453004
Darpan (Andheri)	959	3,273.00	91,644.00	6321019
Deepak (Delisle Road)	819	2,203.00	61,684.00	4973399
Deep [illegible]	[illegible]	2,61[illegible]	[illegible]	[illegible]
Diamond (Borivli)	538	2,255.50	63,154.00	6051116
Dreamland	1033	5,608.00	1,17,768.00 (21 shows)	352066
Dreamland (matinees)	—	3,667.50	25,672.50	352066
Edward	509	961.20	26,914.00	312109
Eros	1024	7,350.03	2,05,801.00	222335
Farhan (Bhiwandi)	763	1,957.10	54,798.80	9247622
Gaiety (Bandra)	974	5,533.00	1,54,924.00	6429255
Galaxy (Bandra)	818	4,644.00	1,30,032.00	6426963
Gemini (Bandra)	238	1,428.00	39,984.00	6429255
Ganesh (Lalbaug)	830	2,610.00	73,080.00	4134243
Ganesh (Thana)	945	2,718.20	76,109.60	594444
Geeta (Worli)	922	2,996.75	83,909.00	4924188

TRADE GUIDE * DIWALI ISSUE * 2ND NOVEMBER 1991

Well, we were able to recover about 70% of our investments on the table through our various minimum guarantee of theatrical rights, audio rights and overseas rights.

With overseas rights, we could recover a significant amount, which gave us the highest pre-release revenues.
Nirnayak box office collections suffered because of 3 reasons:

1. **Censor Board awarding it A Certificate despite of our repeated requests to award a UA certificate (the unpredictable Censor Board) Watch NIRNAYAK and decide for yourself Did NIRNAYAK deserve an A Certificate?)**
2. **Film being released in the month of Ramadan which began on 30th December 1997. (Incidentally there were 2 Ramadan months in the year 1997. This phenomenon happens every 33 years. Next it will happen in the year 2030) You lose at least 30% of theatre audience during this period. Khans, Kapoors, Devgans, Akshay kumar never release their films during this period. We had no other options because theatres were booked by super stars during other periods.**
3. **Under reporting of box office collections by our distributors.**

We got the feedback that the film was doing very good business even after the month of Ramadan.
Even after four weeks, it was doing good business, particularly in the eastern UP region, Bihar, Bengal region.

It was doing very good business even in Nizam, but our distributors were not giving us the correct box office sales.

We talked to the trade pundits what to do and they suggested that if you want real box office sales figures, you announce your next film with a superstar.

Just pay him a signing amount and then you will get the correct numbers because these same distributors will approach you since they are making money with NIRNAYAK, they will approach you to get the distribution rights of your next film.

Also, we were approached by certain agencies who keep a track record.

They've got their agents on all cinema halls across India and they said that we will provide you the correct box office figures, sales figures, ticket sales figures so that then you can sue or fight with your distributors for giving the incorrect sales figures. How reliable were they?

By that time, we were so exhausted having started in 1991 and now successfully being able to release in 1997-98 that did we didn't want to go into any other dispute.

We were happy that the firm ultimately had a decent release.

We have recovered about 70% of our investments and also the worldwide negative rights are with us.
That is with me and my Co producer Shyam Bagaria.

We hold the worldwide negative rights of Nirnayak and Nirnayak being a cult classic, the only Om Puri versus Amrish Puri, the Clash of Titans films, I know that it holds a lot of

long-term value in terms of the market, brand value of the film.

Just to share that quite some time later our Bombay, our Bengal distributor, Bihar Nepal distributor, CP Barar distributor and Delhi UP distributor, they confided in us that they did make money out of Nirnayak distribution and asked us when we plan to launch our next film and they would be interested to take the distribution rights of the next film also.

All said and done, we believe that Nirnayak was a very good film, a great box office success.

And as you can see, its IMDB score of 7/10 is also excellent.

On you tube NIRNAYAK has been viewed by more than 16 lakhs viewers with rave reviews.

I am proud of it and I love Nirnayak my baby.

Box office scam Busted

Exposed 🔥

(1) **Potential Box office collection**

(no of screens x no of seats x price per ticket) **Never declared**

(2) **Actual box office collection** (no of screens x no of tickets sold x selling price of tickets) **Always manipulated**

(3) **False Overstating** of box office collection data

(4) **Self buying of Tickets by rich super stars through corporate route to keep their brand value intact**

(5) **Ticket prices jacked 4X** for the opening weekend.
(6) **Social media Influencers** taking money to promote false sales numbers
(7) **Paradoxically Nirnayak suffered from underreporting of Box Office sales figures by distributors**

CHAPTER 36

Take Home Message

1.Commercial cinema, also called Cinema for Profit, is all about making money and **therefore before you write even the first word of the script, you have to have the entire financial plan in place**, including the budget of the film, why a particular star cast, the cost of making and the various source of returns, profits and income.

2. **So, work out the financials, most important** source of funding, source of returns before even writing down the first word.

3. **It's all about networking**, networking and networking.

I happened to attend screen writing five-day workshop by Uttar Pradesh Film Development Council which was organized by Jaya Bachchan, Krishna Shah and Govind Nihalani where Krishna Shah taught us all about the art and science of film screen writing.

And he said that carry your visiting card in your pocket and just distribute it right, left and center.

Everything is about networking and networking and networking.

Network with the prominent fund providers, prominent producers, prominent directors, prominent actors, prominent writers and film makers.

4. **The shooting part of the film should be finished preferably in a single schedule, start to finish**. Take two years, take three years to write the script, location hunting, to write, the budget, everything.

And once everything about pre-production done and the film goes on floor, finish the shooting in the next 60-90 days, the single stretch start to finish.

You should have the funds.

Everything worked out perfectly.

It keeps the distributors, and exhibitors' confidence on top that they will get a delivery in the next six months.

It prevents lot of possible mishaps like accidents or maybe adverse situations which are beyond control to be minimized.

5. **Always plan for outstation shootings and not in main Bombay because** when the actors and entire crew are shooting in Bombay, they are also preoccupied with their family

problems. Actor may be doing two shift three shift 3 roles simultaneously.
He might be doing a comedy character, he might be doing negative character, he might be doing adventure character and when he has to enter into a character of different types then he is confused and not able to give their full performance.

So, when you take the actor outstation shooting, he remains in that particular mood of a particular character and therefore the performance is relatively very good.

And of course, you when you go out of station shooting the crew is smaller, the technicians you have to work with are less in number in the department of camera, lights, sound and other departments and therefore the cost reduces.

The travelling cost and other boarding and lodging may be higher, but when it offsets with the other expense you save on.

Because the entire crew is in a hurry, they want to go back to Bombay or their hometown with their family. They are willing to work 1 1/2 shift or two shifts, maybe 12 hours 14 hours or 16 hours a day and finish the shoot.

And it improves the performance.

It reduces the interest cost and other burdens and risks.

6. **Try to reduce the possible chances of your main actor becoming a flop.**

Maybe by the time you complete the film ready for release he gives two consecutive flops; nobody will be ready to buy your film. The distributors might just back out of the project.

So, prefer a two-hero film script so that if one hero does not perform good and his released films flop then you can reduce his role and the other hero maybe whose films are released and are super hit and blockbusters, his role is increased.

By increasing the role, screen presence and publicity of the hit hero, by the time your film is ready it is hot and you are able to recover the money on the table and you are able to make money on the overflow after which after the cutting of expenses of the distributor, exhibitor and publicity, other expenses what is called as the overflow you get a share overflow.

7. **The day-to-day shooting requirements need to be worked out in details.**
You go to a location and then you forget something you have not bought which is a very important thing. (The cockroach story)

As I talked about that, out of the 50 things we needed, we forgot to take the cockroaches which was the most important part of the scene and then it took over 4 hours or half of the shift to get it.

We lost time and money.

8. **When you take an actor, is he worth the fee he is asking for?**
You have to understand that when it is about a theatrical release,

what does the actor bring on the table. His fees depends on his crowd pull?

What is his value in the market so that people come to watch him on Friday, Saturday and Sunday, which is the artists pull.

People go to the theatre because of two things.

One is called the artist or the **star pull.**
And then the most important thing becomes the **content pull.**

Initially they will go to the theatre to watch an actor. But ultimately after three days when the news spreads about the film, it is the content which determines the box office collections.

If the news spread that the film is a very nice film, the content is great, then it picks up.

As I mentioned earlier beware of the Star fees. A 6 crore Amitabh Bachchan actually ends up costing 12 crores. With a battery of his team to be paid including the boy, driver, makeup man (Rs 1.5 lakhs per day), social media professionals costing another 6 crores by the time the film is complete.!!!

Also beware of the Star manager or secretary who creates misunderstanding between the actor on one side and the producer, director on the other side, taking advantage of lack of direct communication between them. We faced this problem with the secretary of Kamal Sadanah and when Kamal smelled foul play on part of his secretary he immediately dismissed him from the job.

However, in the coming years the content will become the star, the king, and whosoever is acting become irrelevant and the content of the film will become the real hero.

9. Another point is that because we are now being awarded the **industry status, bank finances** are also available for making the film.

Then **insurance coverage** is very important.

Insurance of the sets which you are making also the insurance of the key actors, life, who are in your movies and maybe the other important crucial things which you are employing need to be insured and covered up.

The staff is covered up so that if somebody gets injured during the shooting then he gets the money for his medical and other expenses.

Lot of films involve special effects these days.

Lot of film involved animation and they also have a major portion in the budget of the film.

Then another thing is that now the cinematographic film or the Kodak film.
Is over. The film is shot digitally.

It ends the cost of the cinematographic film and you can have a repeat shots on the digital camera and see them anywhere and then reshoot the portion with which you feel you can go forward and backward to check before OK.

Otherwise, when it was the era of cinematographic films that once you saw the rushes of the scenes were short and there were certain deficiencies then you had to go back and reshoot certain portions which is called patchwork.

And this patchwork required a lot of finances, lot of planning, a lot of money, the continuity effect and a lot of other things.

10. **Other thing which I have not touched upon is about the role of OTT platforms.**

Now that other options are available, you can make films or web series for the OTT platforms like Amazon, Netflix.

11. **The Pan India South Indian actors likes of Prabhas, Jr NTR, Ram Charan, Allu Arjun, Yash, Vijay are taking over hindi cinema by releasing bilingual, multilingual films. The South Film industry is more receptive to experimental content and varied themes. Films can be made and released in South. South Film industry has preserved the vedic culture and folk culture which is evident in their screen plays and dialogues.**

12. **Then recently the role of artificial intelligence is also coming up.**

So newer and newer techniques and technologies are coming up which are affecting the art and science of filmmaking and these have these have to be taken into account while you are making a film for the commercial market for the purpose of profit, for the purpose of money-making money from the films.

CHAPTER 37

What next?

As I have discussed that a commercial film production is all about money, it's all about cinema for profit.

And as I understand there are three ways one can enter into commercial film production.

One is that they have a contract with the OTT platforms like Amazon, Netflix, Hotstar.

They already have a fixed budget which they give you to produce a film.

You make the film and give it to them and make whatever profit out of it.

The 2nd way is whether it is a production house for theatre or a film or web series for OTT platforms like Amazon, Netflix, Hotstar.

You set up a project. You have a script.

You sign the saleable actor, You sign the saleable director, You sign the cameraman. You sign the various technicians, the basic team.

You sign everyone to make a readily launchable project of which the shooting can start as early as possible.

And once you have completed this setup, you sell it to some production house or OTT platform.

This is the second way.

The third, of course, is that you make the complete film in a certain budget and then you show it to different OTT platforms or production houses for release either on in the theatre or directly on the OTT platform.

These are the three ways as of today, and one important way of approaching a film as a producer is that either you are in touch with a saleable actor or a saleable director or established production house.

Either of the three and you have a script with you.
You tie up your If you're saleable actor likes the script, then the film finances and the entire crew will be set up.

If the saleable director likes the script, then of course again the funds can be arranged and the entire crew can be set up.

And of course, if a production house likes your script, then also the entire team, the director, the actor and the entire crew can be set up.

And of late the OTT platform is also a big option apart from theatrical release, one can directly release on OTT.

But as I told you about the nepotism which is there, and the Vaishwaad which is there in the Bollywood, where certain families control Bollywood, the Khans, the Kapoors, the the Bachchan's, the Akhtars, the Devgans control the film industry.

And it is very difficult to go around these production houses, the Khan productions, the Kapoor productions, Akhtar Productions, Devgan Productions, Akshay Kumar Productions, Puja Bhatt Productions, Balaji Telefilms. It is very difficult to bypass them, pierce them and go around them, **even on the OTT platforms.**

I'm aware that there are certain people interested in producing commercial films. They've got the funds, they've got the scripts, they've got the actors and the directors.

But then even for the OTT, the entire OTT is booked by these production houses of Khans, Kapoors, Devgans and Akhtars.

And if you have to even go to the OTT platform for a web series or a film, you have to go through these production houses and as usual they take the cream of the profits and the income and you will just get maybe a simple interest on the money which you have put in and maybe some kind of a credit or Co producer.

That is my understanding, that things need to change in future so that real talent, real content, real actors is able to reach the top.

Another issue which I have already said is that when I attended a 5-day workshop on screenplay writing, which was organized by UP Film Development Council and Jaya Bachchan was a chairperson. Krishna Shah and Govind Nihalani. Krishna Shah who made films in Hollywood stress the importance of networking, networking and networking.

Keep on networking with directors, with producers, with screen writers, with actors and you will surely get a breakthrough.

People ask me that after the success of Nirnayak, why didn't you make another film after the successful release?

And my answer is very simple that I had seen very closely the nepotism, the Vanshwaad and the control of insiders in Bollywood.

And I realized that it will be very difficult for me as either I work under them or if I want to be an independent producer, director, writer, it is very difficult to fight against these powerful lobbies.

That was in the late 1990s, but I think with the entry of the OTT platforms like Amazon, Netflix and now that the South Indian cinema is simultaneously releasing multilingual films and also simultaneously releasing it in Hindi, there is a bigger scope for outsiders.

I think the canvas has become bigger for aspiring outsider screenwriters, directors, producers and there are options, which I will also research and try to find out in South Indian cinema, which appears to be giving chance to budding producers, writers, directors.

A big example of today is the success of Kantara, which was a small budget film of 10 to 12 crores and made a box office success of 400 crores.

I think there are ways outsiders can really fight this Nepotism, Vanshwad and control of insiders and become a successful commercial film producer.

But one thing is sure, that nepotism, Vanshwad and insider control and exploitation has to end, and real talent of India gets a level playing field, if Indian Cinema has to beat Hollywood in terms of content and revenue.

CHAPTER 38

Bollywood Past Present Future

Indian cinema Past, Present and future.

Bollywood, the so-called the Hindi Cinema, has never truly represented the socio-cultural texture of the Hindi belt which includes the Uttar Pradesh, Madhya Pradesh, Rajasthan, Haryana since its early times from 1930 to 1960.

Because the **Marathis** played a major role in developing the Hindi cinema, these 30 years **from 1930 to 1960** were dominated by the Marathi culture, the Maharashtrian culture.

Most of the films represented that culture.

This was taken over between **1960 to 1990 by the Bengali** film makers Satyajit Ray, Basu Bhattacharya, Rishikesh Mukherjee as in saying so, it was more a representation of the Bengali culture.

And then came 1990s.

The Punjabis and the Khans, as their children, the insider kids, the star kids were coming up.

From 1990 onwards, with Karan Johar, Aditya Chopra coming up, it was more a representative of a Punjabi culture, the Khan culture, and they were also promoting more of the Western culture between 1990 and 2020 and Indian culture, the Hindu Sanatan expression through Hindi films took a back seat.

In fact, they played a major part in destroying the traditional Indian socio-cultural environment.

But during this same time, the South Indian, the Tamil cinema, the Telugu Cinema, the Malayalam cinema, the Kannada cinema they kept the Hindu culture, Hindu Sanatan culture alive through their films which were more made in the South Indian languages.

And after three months, six months they were dubbed in Hindi and we could watch them on certain TV channels only after 6 months of their theatrical release in south. Hindi Dubbed versions of South Indian cinema to be simultaneously released multilingually was not a trend. And actors like Ajay Devgan, Akshay Kumar, Khans, Kapoors took advantage of this situation, bought the hindi rights of the hit south Indian movies and minted money. There were no original great screen writers left in Bollywood.

But Baahubali in 2020 changed the entire concept.

Baahubali a South Indian cinema was released in multilingual languages including Hindi and it did great business.

And the trend of South Indian cinema or films simultaneously being dubbed or made in Hindi and released all over India now became popular.

The actual Pan India superstars of the likes of Prabhas, NTR junior, Ram Charan, Yash, Allu Arjun, Vijay were born. These South Indian Super Stars are Real Life Heroes too. Real Leaders. Look at NTR, Jaylalitha and recently Pawan Kalyan. Not only have they entered politics but successfully floated their own political parties. Suresh Gopi has become the first BJP Lok Sabha MP from Kerala. Real life heroes all of them!!! And these Bollywood nepotism, vanshwadi, insiders just concentrated on how to destroy the careers of talented outsiders.

Then these south Indian superstars who represent Pan India came into play and they dominating the Bollywood stars whose film following was just restricted to northern part of India because of the below average content of films they made. **Now the Bollywood Stars are forced to do villain or supporting roles in such South Indian movies.!!!**

A lot of Ajay Devgan, Akshay Kumar, Shahrukh Khan films are the remakes of the South Indian Super hit films. Now this has stopped due to simultaneous multilingual releases of South Indian films.

That culture ended because now the South Indian films are directly being released in Hindi and this is the trend which started in 2020 and could continue for till 2050 because they are also representing the Hindu Sanatan culture which is on the revival and restoration phase.

But one more thing which we are seeing is that the epicentre of the Hindi cinema appears to be shifting towards Noida Yamuna Expressway film city which is the dream child of the Chief Minister of Uttar Pradesh Yogi Adityanath.

And who feels that Hindi cinema, the epicentre of Hindi cinema, should be in the somewhere in the Hindi belt and from where the Hindi films are made, produced and the content is to be made here.

There is a shift from Bombay towards Yamuna Expressway, Noida Film City and I think that would be followed pan India. We have very little North-East presence in terms of content, in terms of actors.

The period between 1990 and 2020 has been dominated by the Punjabi actors. The Khans and the Kapoors have dominated this period.

We have never seen a single non-Khan, non-Kapoor or non-Punjabi actor since 1990 in the top ten Bollywood actors. No one from Bihar, Haryana, UP, Madhya Pradesh, J&K or South India.

But this appears to be changing and in the futures we will be witnessing the Pan India superstars of South and hopefully outsiders from the Hindi belt occupying the Top 10 Bollywood heroes list.

Why are the Khans and Kapoors and the Punjabi actors resisting non-Punjabi and non Khan so-called the outsiders from entering the top ten Bollywood actors is evident? Because 80% of the profits of the revenues of the film goes to these top ten actors.

They are charging fees to the tune of 30-80 crores per film and they do not want any outsiders to get that kind of money.

But things are changing and hopefully with the South Indian pan india actor showing the way, we would have more actors, revival of the Bengali cinema actors, revival of the Marathi cinema actors. The North Indian outsiders should also make their presence as super stars.

As we know Assam chief minister is making big strides in in promoting films in in the northeast which should be visible over the 10 to 12 years.

So this is, I believe, is the entire journey of Hindi cinema from 1930s to maybe the next 50 to 100 years.

CHAPTER 39

I Cherish a Dream

Bollywood defeating Hollywood.

I cherish a dream of Bollywood beating Hollywood in terms of the quality of content, box office collections, the total revenue collections worldwide.

Bharat is a land of storytellers.

More than 100 plus crore people have many stories to tell.

It is the land where important messages, important lessons to people of all ages were transmitted through the Pancha Tantra stories, the Puranas and other Vedic scriptures where you learned about life, managing life, leading a successful life through illustrations and stories mentioned in the Vedic scriptures.

We Indians, when four friends sit together over a cup of tea, never realize while we are talking, sharing stories, gossiping on various issues, how 4-5 hours have passed, as the time flies by so fast. India is a community of people who love sharing stories.

But these stories, good stories, good content has to reach the top and be converted into cinema, these real-life stories need a chance.

The hindrance to this quality is the nepotism, Vanshwaad, the control and exploitation by the insiders of the outsiders, at the top end of Hindi cinema Bollywood.

And unless and until the talent of India, which is the top writers, directors, producers and in particularly the outsider actors enter the top ten and create the best of cinema content, it would be difficult for Hindi cinema, Indian cinema, Bollywood to counter the films of Hollywood.

It is my dream, a dream I cherish that one day, like in Indian politics, Indian cricket, nepotism, vanshwad and exploitation by insiders is ending. In the same way Bollywood will be free of nepotism and the real all India talent, talented actors, talented film makers, talented directors, talented screenwriters are able to express themselves and without hindrance or obstruction reach top 10.

CHAPTER 40

Cut To ..... 24′

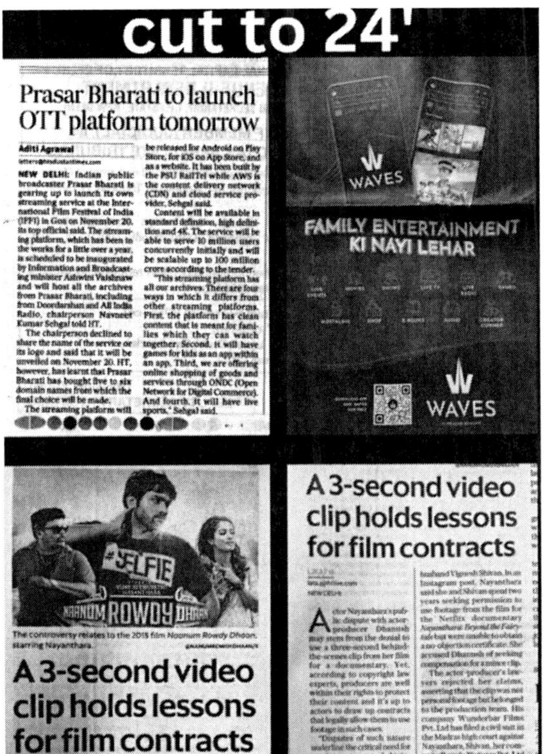

Prasar Bharati to launch OTT platform tomorrow

Aditi Agrawal

letters@hindustantimes.com

NEW DELHI: Indian public broadcaster Prasar Bharati is gearing up to launch its own streaming service at the International Film Festival of India (IFFI) in Goa on November 20, its top official said. The streaming platform, which has been in the works for a little over a year, is scheduled to be inaugurated by Information and Broadcasting minister Ashwini Vaishnaw and will host all the archives from Prasar Bharati, including from Doordarshan and All India Radio, chairperson Navneet Kumar Sehgal told HT.

The chairperson declined to share the name of the service or its logo and said that it will be unveiled on November 20. HT, however, has learnt that Prasar Bharati has bought five to six domain names from which the final choice will be made.

The streaming platform will be released for Android on Play Store, for iOS on App Store, and as a website. It has been built by the PSU RailTel while AWS is the content delivery network (CDN) and cloud service provider, Sehgal said.

Content will be available in standard definition, high definition and 4K. The service will be able to serve 10 million users concurrently initially and will be scalable up to 100 million crore according to the tender.

"This streaming platform has all our archives. There are four ways in which it differs from other streaming platforms. First, the platform has clean content that is meant for families which they can watch together. Second, it will have games for kids as an app within an app. Third, we are offering online shopping of goods and services through ONDC (Open Network for Digital Commerce). And fourth, it will have live sports," Sehgal said.

The controversy relates to the 2015 film *Naanum Rowdy Dhaan*, starring Nayanthara.

A 3-second video clip holds lessons for film contracts

A 3-second video clip holds lessons for film contracts

NEW DELHI

Actor Nayanthara's public dispute with actor-producer Dhanush may stem from the denial to use a three-second behind-the-scenes clip from her film for a documentary. Yet, according to copyright law experts, producers are well within their rights to protect their content and it's up to actors to draw up contracts that legally allow them to use footage in such cases.

"Disputes of such nature underline the critical need for precise contracts and obtain-

husband Vignesh Shivan. In an Instagram post, Nayanthara said she and Shivan spent two years seeking permission to use footage from the film for the Netflix documentary *Nayanthara: Beyond the Fairy-tale* but were unable to obtain a no objection certificate. She accused Dhanush of seeking compensation for a minor clip.

The actor-producer's lawyers rejected her claims, asserting that the clip was not personal footage but belonged to the production team. His company Wunderbar Films Pvt. Ltd has filed a civil suit in the Madras high court against Nayanthara, Shivan, her company Rowdy Pictures Pvt. Ltd

WITH BIG-BUDGET MOVIES BOMBING...

More Films Shelved as Bollywood Stops Shooting for Stars

Fading star power, high fee make films unviable; changing audience tastes also a reason: Producers

Rajesh N Naidu

Covid Rewrites B'wood Script

How the cost of film-making has changed post-pandemic

Actors' remuneration increased to 50-60% of budget, from 40-50% pre-Covid

Fee of mid-range actors has jumped three times

A-list actors demand three vanity vans—one each for workout, food and their entourage

Technicians' fee jumped two times as they shift from web series to movies

Behind that fading Hindi movie magic

Kunal Ray

[THE WAY WE WERE]

Poonam Saxena

Can I have a katha or kahani, please?

Malls may Cut Multiplex Space as Cinema-led Revenues Shrink

Streaming platforms, high ticket prices, poor box office performance key reasons

Faizan Haidar & Rajesh N Naidu

The Multiplex Tragedy

Lack of business sense in multiplexes due to:

- Increasing acceptance of streaming platforms
- High ticket prices in multiplexes
- Weak scripts and resultant poor performance at the box office

Box office collection:

End of 2023: ₹13,161 crore

For 2024 till date: ₹7,811.8 crore

AI Use Comes of Age in Hindi Film Production

From storyboarding to deaging, new-age tools can save up to 30% of costs

Wearing Several Caps

FOR FULL REPORT, GO TO WWW.ECONOMICTIMES.COM

Vaishnaw urges stronger curbs on social media, OTT content

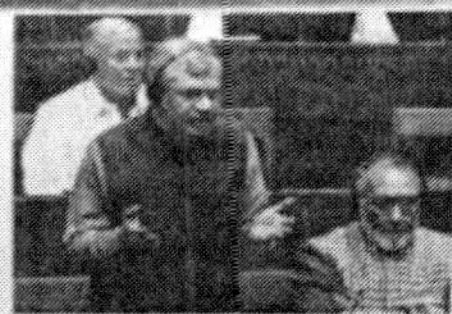

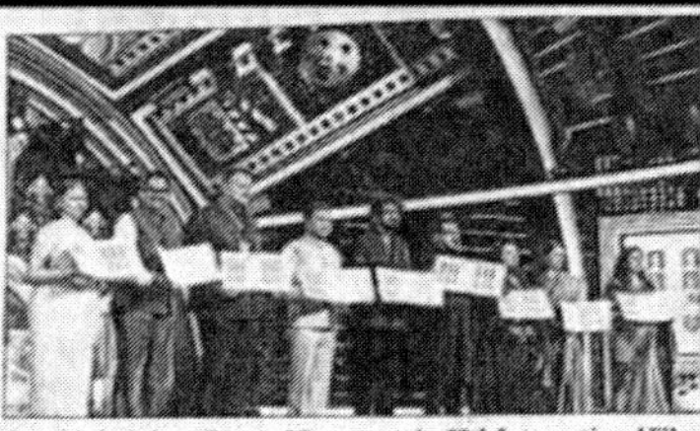

Goa chief minister Pramod Sawant at the 55th International Film Festival of India in Goa on Wednesday. PTI

Keen to develop content creators' economy: Min

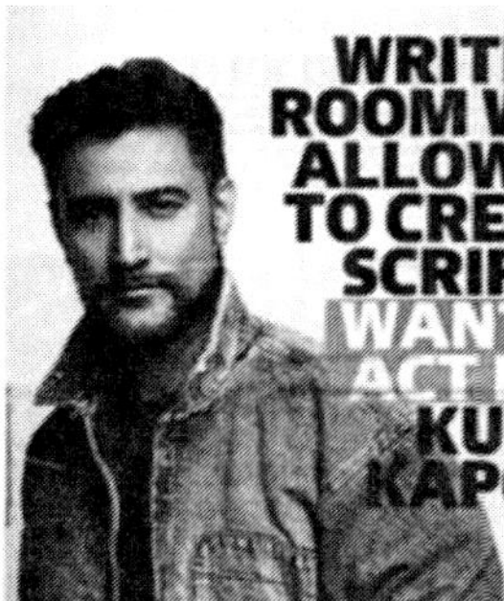

WRITER'S ROOM WILL ALLOW ME TO CREATE SCRIPTS I WANT TO ACT FOR: KUNAL KAPOOR

The Multiplex Tragedy

Lack of business sense in multiplexes due to:

- **Increasing acceptance** of streaming platforms
- **High ticket** prices in multiplexes
- **Weak scripts** and resultant poor performance at the box office

Box office collection:

End of 2023: ₹13,161 crore

For 2024 till date: ₹7,811.8 crore

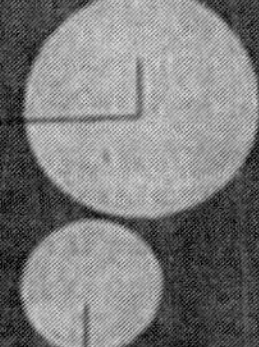

(Sacnilk)

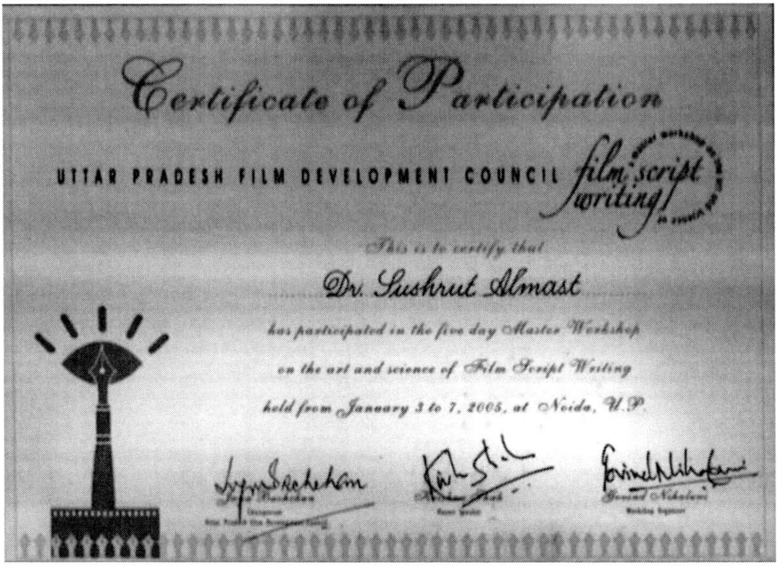
Certificate of Participation

UTTAR PRADESH FILM DEVELOPMENT COUNCIL

film script writing

This is to certify that

Dr. Sushrut Almast

has participated in the five day Master Workshop

on the art and science of Film Script Writing

held from January 3 to 7, 2005, at Noida, U.P.

Amidst the Insider-Outsider cold war a few facts which have emerged over the last decade:

(1) **OTT platforms** have given opportunity for all India talent to expose and express itself.
(2) **North South divide** of Indian cinema is fast dissolving.
(3) **Post Bahubali** success South Film makers are directly releasing their films dubbed in Hindi simultaneously worldwide. Ajay Devgan's and Akshay Kumar not getting to make remakes of hit south films in Hindi.

(4) **PAN Indian Actors are emerging from south** with the names of likes of Prabhas, Allu Arjun, Yash, NTR Junior, Ram Charan, Thalapathy Vijay becoming household names in Northern, Eastern and Western parts of India

(5) **Era of King Khans and King Kapoor's is ending**

(6) **Content is fast becoming the new King.**
(7) **Stories inspired from real life are taking over**

(8) **History is being told through Cinema**

(9) **Technology is showing its potential** in an astronomical way

But one thing which has always disturbed me is our great actors & acting brands going waste, underutilized.

The talented heroes and heroines having a life span of 15 to 25 years, go into oblivion, only to emerge as father or mother after 15 years. **We don't still write stories with our brand actors as main protagonists in 60 plus age group. Talent of likes of Dharmendra, Vinod Khanna, Sachin, Amol Palekar have gone to waste. Talent of likes of Sharmila Tagore, Hema Malini, Rekha has not been utilized properly.**

The only actor who has been able to establish this idiom "Once a Hero, Always a Hero" is Amitabh Bachchan, all thanks to the screen writers and directors who have been writing and making films with Amitabh Bachchan as the main protagonist. As Bachchan Sr has always said what he is today is because of the stories he got.

Also, it is my firm conviction that if writers from science, commerce and arts background sit together to work on a story great scripts can be created.

Films cities should be developed with the concept of "Come with an idea, go home with a released film." This is possible if all stake holders and intermediaries work from the same campus. Screen writers clubs are created and Screen writers block with chambers and offices allotted to screen writers for brain storming sessions and master scripts.

BCCI – Board for Control of Cinema in India with state chapters and interstate cinema competitions can unearth hidden talent across India take India – the country of story tellers to its zenith.

And as the proverb goes "Be the change you want to see"

I have written and am in the process of penning commercial film scripts where the main protagonist is sixty plus years of age.

Hope India and the world gets to see the great story telling talent that India is!!!

The recent developments:
"Malls may cut Multiplex Space as Cinema led Revenues shrink."

"AI Use Comes of Age in Hindi Film Production."

Ä 3-second video clip holds lessons for film contracts."

"Keen to develop content creators' economy: Min"

"Prasar Bharati to launch OTT platform "WAVES" tomorrow."

"Writer's" Room will allow me to create scripts.

"Vaishnav urges stronger curbs on social media, OTT content."

"Can I have a Katha or Kahani please."

"Behind that fading Hindi Movie magic."

More Films Shelved as Bollywood Stops Shooting for Stars."

Stand testimony to the facts that

"Khan is not king; content is king."

No individual, a khan, a kapoor, a bachchan, a bhatt, a devgan or a akhtar is bigger than the nation, industry (Bollywood) or the organization, he or she represents. We are all here to create a better nation, a better industry, a better organization we represent.

The time for success of Bollywood outsiders has arrived.

We will soon see an outsider Rs 50 Crore per film hero.!!!

And as I am finishing the final editing of Bollywood Outsider – A Success Story, the Hindi-dubbed version of Pushpa 2 – The Rule is spreading like a wildfire across the Hindi Belt and in the process creating all new bollywood box office records!!!

LIST OF ILLUSTRATIONS AND PHOTOS

24	16	Liberty Shoes Force 10 In Film Advertising Contract
25	16	In film advertisement of Force 10 songs & Motor Cycle
26	17	Film censorship requirements
27	17	Cuts proposed by Censor Board
28	17	Censor Board issues Censor Certificate with A rating
29	17	Censorship : Publicity material
30	18	Trishna Ghai complaint to The Cine Artists Association
31	18	Bappi lahiri music director signs in
32	18	Om Puri signs in
33	18	Kamal Sadanah removes his secretary for misinformation
34	20	Distributor Contract - Nepal
35	20	Distributor Contract - Overseas
36	20	Nirnayak Audio Contract - Ultra
37	22	Print Publicity -Trade Magazines Pre release
38	22	Print Publicity - In Theatres photo Sets
39	24	Camera, Lights, Lens Bill
40	27	Press Publicity: Kamal Sadanah, Indrani Banerjee, Trishna
41	27	Press Publicity: Kamal Sadanah, Indrani Banerjee, Trishna
42	28	Kamal Sadanah Lab Letter
43	28	kamal Sadanah forgoes dues against Lab Letter
44	28	Amrish Puri Lab Letter
45	28	Indrani Banerjee forgoes dues against Lab Letter
46	34	Divya Dutta Contract
47	34	Divya Dutta Contract
48	35	Nirnayak - Collection Statement by Distributor
49	35	Monitoring Box Office - Raiding Agencies
50	35	Amitabh Bachchan ABCL - A production Disaster

51	35	List of All India Theatres and capacities
52	40	Prasar Bharati launches OTT Platform WAVES
53	40	Big Budget Bollywood Hindi Movies Shelved
54	40	Fading magic of Bollywood Hindi Films
55	40	Film Producer Sushrut Almast turns Film Screen Writer